R=AL
SKILLS BOOK
1
ANGELIKA BRUNEL

REAL ENGLISH AUTHENTIC LEARNING

SPÉCIMEN

CHENELIÈRE
ÉDUCATION

**REAL, Real English Authentic Learning
Skills Book 1**

Angelika Brunel

© 2009 Chenelière Education Inc.

Editor: Melissa Repas
Project Managers: Amanda Kelly, Majorie Perreault,
  Rebecca Schwarz
Researchers: Rachel Irwin, Amanda Kelly, Marie-Chantal Laforge,
  Majorie Perreault
Copy Editors: Vicky Bell, Kevin Polesello, Rebecca Schwarz
Proofreaders: Amanda Kelly, Veronica Schami, David Turpie
Illustrator: Volta
Cover and Book Designer: Andrée Lauzon
Printer: Imprimeries Transcontinental

Development and authoring of Odilon's online exercises:
Patti Holter

**Bibliothèque et Archives nationales du Québec and
Library and Archives Canada cataloguing in publication**

Brunel, Angelika, 1965-

REAL, Real English Authentic Learning. Skills Book 1

Includes bibliographical references.
For college students.

ISBN 978-2-7650-2232-9

1. English language – Textbooks for second language
learners.   2. English language – Spoken English – Problems,
exercises, etc.   3. English language – Problems, exercises, etc.
I. Title.

PE1128.B78 2009   428.3'4   C2009-940875-9

**CHENELIÈRE
ÉDUCATION**

7001 Saint Laurent Blvd.
Montréal (Québec) Canada H2S 3E3
Telephone: 514 273-1066
Fax: 450 461-3834 / 1 888 460-3834
info@cheneliere.ca

ISBN 978-2-7650-2232-9

Dépôt légal : 2e trimestre 2009
Bibliothèque et Archives nationales du Québec
Bibliothèque et Archives Canada

Printed in Canada

1 2 3 4 5 ITIB 13 12 11 10 09

We acknowledge the financial support of the Government of
Canada through the Book Publishing Industry Development
Program (BPIDP) for our publishing activities.

Acknowledgements

I would first like to thank the marvelous team at Chenelière Education for making this book
possible. Many thanks to all those, too numerous to name, who sacrificed long hours to
ensure the best possible results. I would also like to thank Kay Powell, my colleague and
the author of the accompanying Real Grammar Book, for being a great accomplice along
the way! Finally, this book would not be what it is without the continual guidance and careful
supervision of our editor, Melissa Repas, whose watchful eye never let us settle for less
than the very best. Thank you.

Heartfelt thanks and sincere appreciation to all the reviewers who praised, challenged,
offered insight, and fine-tuned the production of this book.

Chinlee Choo Foo, Collège de Maisonneuve   Charles Lapointe, Cégep de Sainte-Foy
Izabela Kubinska, Collège de Valleyfield   Rachel Tunnicliffe, Collège Merici

Thank you to Patti Holter for authoring such a fabulous online resource for Odilon.

I dedicate this book to my loving son Richard, my greatest fan and my source of inspiration.

Photo Credits

p. III: Greg Epperson/iStockphoto; **p. X (top):** Juriah Mosin/Shutterstock, **p. X (centre):** Vernon Wiley/
iStockphoto, **p. X (bottom):** Quavondo Nguyen/iStockphoto; **p. XI (left):** © Corbis Super RF/Alamy,
p. XI (right): Kristian Sekulic/Shutterstock; **p. 1:** © Dan Vincent/Alamy; **p. 2:** © Jeff Greenberg/Alamy;
p. 4-5: gracieuseté de Cunard Line; **p. 6:** © Ron Yue/Alamy; **p. 8:** Alexey Stiop/iStockphoto; **p. 11:**
Quavondo Nguyen/iStockphoto; **p. 13:** Hagit Berkovich/Shutterstock; **p. 14:** Juriah Mosin/Shutterstock;
p. 15: Christoph Weihs/Shutterstock; **p. 18:** © Randy Faris/Corbis; **p. 19:** Alan Becker/Getty Images;
p. 21: Arthur Kwiatkowski/iStockphoto; **p. 23 (left):** Rod Ferris/Shutterstock, **(centre):** BORTEL Pavel/
Shutterstock, **(right):** Adam Tinney/Shutterstock; **p. 25:** Lee Pettet/iStockphoto; **p. 26 (top):** Quavondo
Nguyen/iStockphoto, **(centre):** Gert Vrey/iStockphoto, **(bottom):** Losevsky Pavel/Shutterstock; **p. 27:**
gracieuseté de asiphoto.com; **p. 29:** Tim Baker; **p. 30:** Charles knox/Shutterstock; **p. 31:** Teresa Pigeon/
iStockphoto; **p. 32:** © Association de Ultimate de Montréal (AUM); **p. 34:** Dawn Weaver/The Pillow
Fight League; **p. 38:** Extremeironing.com; **p. 39:** Joerg Reimann/iStockphoto; **p. 40 (left):** james steidl/
iStockphoto, **(right):** wsfurlan/iStockphoto; **p. 41:** PMSI Web Hosting and Design/iStockphoto; **p. 43:** Rob
Belknap/iStockphoto; **p. 44:** Wojciech Burda/Shutterstock; **p. 47:** Gelpi/Shutterstock; **p. 49:** Frances L. Fruit/
Shutterstock; **p. 51:** Carme Balcells/iStockphoto; **p. 53:** © Corbis Super RF/Alamy; **p. 55:** gracieuseté
de Irobot; **p. 57:** Carolina K. Smith, M.D./Shutterstock; **p. 58:** Michael Bretherton/iStockphoto;
p. 59: Vicki France/Shutterstock; **p. 60:** A. Inden/zefa/Corbis; **p. 62:** Lein de León Yong/Shutterstock;
p. 64: Musée du Québec/Collection Henri Julien; **p. 66:** kwest/Shutterstock; **p. 71:** INTERFOTO
Pressebildagentur/Alamy; **p. 76:** Steven Miric/iStockphoto; **p. 77:** Carmen Martínez/iStockphoto;
p. 78: Wolfgang Amri/iStockphoto; **p. 79:** Masterfile; **p. 81:** Andresr/iStockphoto; **p. 82:** © Markus
Moellenberg/zefa/Corbis; **p. 84:** Trista Weibell/iStockphoto; **p. 86 (1):** Kiselev Andrey Valerevich/
Shutterstock, **(2):** Tammy Bryngelson/iStockphoto, **(3):** Erics/Shutterstock, **(4):** Earl Eliason/iStockphoto,
(5): Daniel Rodriguez/iStockphoto, **(6):** Jason Stitt/iStockphoto, **(7):** Earl Eliason/iStockphoto, **(8):**
Justin Horrocks/iStockphoto; **p. 88:** Alexander Hafemann/iStockphoto; **p. 89:** Andresr/Shutterstock;
p. 91: Corbis/First Light; **p. 92:** Oleg Prikhodko/iStockphoto; **p. 94:** Greg Meeson/hitandrun/Alamy;
p. 95: Vernon Wiley/iStockphoto; **p. 96:** © Bettmann/CORBIS; **p. 98:** DN-Group/iStockphoto; **p. 100:**
Jason Stitt/iStockphoto; **p. 101:** Jon Drews/iStockphoto; **p. 103:** Adrian Wyld/THE CANADIAN PRESS;
p. 104: gracieuseté de The Orange Lounge Recording Company; **p. 107:** Frank van den Bergh/
iStockphoto; **p. 110:** Kristian Sekulic/Shutterstock; **p. 111:** Plainview/iStockphoto; **p. 113:** David Gunn/
iStockphoto; **p. 114:** Bart Coenders/iStockphoto; **p. 115:** iofoto/Shutterstock; **p. 116:** Vinko Murko/
iStockphoto; **p. 117:** Steve Luker/iStockphoto; **p. 119:** Julie Deshaies/iStockphoto; **p. 120:** Andresr/
Shutterstock; **p. 121:** Ericsphotography/iStockphot0; **p. 122:** Leigh Schindler/iStockphoto; **p. 125:**
Marcus Lindström/iStockphoto; **p. 126:** G. Zimbel/PUBLIPHOTO; **p. 130:** Masterfile; **p. 134:** 21TORR
archives GmbH/iStockphoto; **p. 135:** Daniela Andreea Spyropoulos/iStockphoto; **p. 136:** FutureDigital
Design/Christopher Futcher/Big Stock Photo; **p. 137:** Chris Schmidt/iStockphoto; **p. 138:** © Radius
Images/Corbis; **p. 139:** Chris Schmidt/iStockphoto; **p. 142:** Edyta Cholcha-Cisowska/iStockphoto;
p. 143: webphotographeer/iStockphoto; **p. 144:** Chris Schmidt/iStockphoto **and p. 147:** Thomas M
Perkins/Shutterstock.

Author Sources

Unit 3, p. 43: "Strangest Things Ever Sold On eBay: Top 10 Auctions," by Jeff Cohen: business.solve
yourproblem.com/buy-on-ebay/strangest_items_ever_sold_on_ebay.shtml and "Top 10 Strangest eBay
Items Ever Sold": www.onlineauctiontrader.com/ebaybuying21.htm; **p. 44:** "What is a life 4 sale":
www.alife4sale.com and "What is '100 Goals in 100 Weeks'": www.100goals100weeks.com. **Unit 5,
p. 79:** "How to Catch a Liar," by Melanie Lindner, *Forbes:* www.forbes.com/2008/04/02/reid-technique-
lying-ent-manage-cx_ml_0402catchaliar.html and "How to Detect a Lie Signs that someone is not telling
the truth," by Sandra Williams behavioural-psychology.suite101.com/article.cfm/how_to_detect_a_lie.
Unit 6, p. 103: "Skating across cultural gap," by Kevin Allen, *USA TODAY:* www.usatoday.com/sports/
hockey/nhl/predators/2003-07-22-tootoo-cover_x.htm, "Nashville's new face: rookie Jordin Tootoo, the
first native Inuit to play in the NHL, is winning over the Music City faithful," by Anthony Stoeckhert,
Hockey Digest: findarticles.com/p/articles/mi_m0FCM/is_3_32/ai_112087319, "Profile: Who is
Jordin Tootoo?," *CBC News:* www.cbc.ca/news/background/aboriginals/tootoo_jordin.html and
Jordin Tootoo, *Wikipedia* entry: en.wikipedia.org/wiki/Jordin_Tootoo; **p. 104:** Justin Hines Foundation:
www.justinhines.org and Justin Hines Biography: www.justinhines.com/biography.php. **Unit 7, p. 117:**
"The 7 kids' health myths every mom should ignore," by Rosemary Black, Marguerite Lamb, and
Laura Flynn McCarthy, *Parenting.com:* www.cnn.com/2006/HEALTH/parenting/12/07/par.sick.myths/
index.html and "Myth: Toilet Seats Are the Dirtiest Thing in the Bathroom," *ABC News:* abcnews.go.com/
2020/Health/story?id=1213831.

Member of the CERC

Member of the
*Association nationale
des éditeurs de livres*

CERC
Canadian Educational
Resources Council

ASSOCIATION
NATIONALE
DES ÉDITEURS
DE LIVRES

Introduction

Dear ESL Colleagues,

As the author of **REAL** Skills Book Level 1, I am very proud to introduce this exceptional teaching tool, produced by the committed, qualified, and creative team at Chenelière Education. At first glance, you will probably notice the rich colours and dynamic photos that give this series a unique and magazine-like feel. Yet when you look inside, you will find so much more than its visual appeal.

    REAL offers teachers and students up-to-date and intriguing Canadian content, along with the necessary pedagogical tools needed to ensure the success of **high-beginner to low-intermediate** students.

REAL offers real themes, real structure, and real freedom

The title **REAL** conveys the idea that students want an authentic learning experience. In other words, they want to leave the classroom and be able to function in the real world. Moreover, the word **REAL** is about the value of being real and true to yourself, a concept that resonates with students today.

    The teacher- and student-tested themes in each unit were carefully selected to encourage students to explore **relevant and stimulating issues** that concern them and the world around them. Using an **integrated approach**, **REAL** allows for thorough practice and application of language in each of the four skills. This approach also allows students to generate thoughtful *Discussion* and build **critical thinking skills**, while giving students the **support they need** to complete their learning tasks.

    Although the units are designed with a natural flow of activities, they also offer the **flexibility** to choose the activities that are appropriate for your students. Each unit can span two weeks (as many as three, if you complete the projects), providing you with more than 45 hours of course material. Ultimately, you have the freedom to choose and adapt the material that works best for you and your students. Do consult the teacher's notes for extra ideas on how to adapt or expand activities according to your students' needs.

REAL considers the real needs and interests of high-beginner to low-intermediate students

Great care and attention has been paid to ensure that the pedagogical activities meet the language learning needs and interests of your students. For example, the integrated *Pronunciation* activities target common pronunciation difficulties experienced by beginner-level students, who also still need to acquire a great deal of vocabulary. To meet this goal, the vocabulary words featured in the **vocabulary acquisition** exercises, the *In Words* activities (which supply students with words related to the unit themes) and the *Top Words* section

at the end of each unit, were all carefully selected according to word frequency and usefulness in helping students complete unit tasks. Finally, the captivating *Audio and Video Programs*, the high-interest and level appropriate *reading* material, the fun and motivating *Warm-Up*, and the dynamic *speaking* activities were all researched, chosen, or created for the needs and interests of beginner-level students.

REAL offers real integrated language learning opportunities

Built into each unit are language learning skills and **strategies** that students need to become more efficient and effective language learners. These are found in the *How to…* boxes throughout the book, greatly supporting students in their speaking and writing tasks. Additionally, special attention is paid to **integrating grammar** into each unit's communication activities. This **focus on form approach** has been proven to increase language accuracy and retention of grammatical structures. *Language Link* boxes explain the grammar rule needed to complete the speaking or writing task at hand, before directing students to the accompanying grammar book for more detailed explanations and practice. Finally, the *Writing Files* section, integrated into each unit to reinforce learning, breaks down the writing process into manageable steps, starting at the sentence level. This section can be referred to at any time, and is on beige pages for easy reference.

REAL offers real opportunities to creatively reuse and recycle the language learned

I encourage you to use the *Project Files* section at the end of each unit throughout the semester. It includes fun, creative, and motivating theme-related speaking and writing projects that allow students to review, integrate, and practise the vocabulary, strategies and grammar learned in the unit. These also allow students to review and practise the unit themes, and give **confidence** to use them beyond the classroom. The accompanying *Review, Recycle, Remember* box helps students focus on what they have learned in the unit and encourages them to reapply this knowledge in their projects. Lastly, the *Reference Section* is a great support for speaking and writing tasks. Before completing projects, students can consult it for necessary strategies, such as producing effective and cohesive paragraphs, avoiding plagiarism, and selecting reliable sources.

I am confident that **REAL** is a teaching tool that will more than adequately support your students as they endeavour to improve their English.

Wishing you a successful and rewarding semester!

Angelika Brunel
Collège Ahuntsic

Features

Opening Page

A **magazine-style look** offering **up-to-date themes** allows you to explore issues related to your everyday life and the world around you.

Thought-provoking questions introduce the topic of the unit.

A theme-related **idiom** gives you real English expressions.

How Do You Want to See the
WORLD?

Latest trends give travellers more OPTIONS

Is it possible to combine work and travel?

What are some options for budget travel?

What impact does travel have on the environment?

In this unit, you will explore the different options you have to see the world.

UNIT 1

ON THE GO!

YOUR ONLINE COMPANION

What is Odilon?

For the student

A stimulating virtual tool allowing:

- Online learning through diverse and stimulating activities

- Immediate feedback and scoring to help better assess understanding of the subject matter and to monitor progress

For the teacher

A strong student-management tool allowing:

- Access to numerous activities to use in class, in the lab, for homework, or to monitor progress through student evaluation

- Automatic correction, saving valuable time by organizing students' results in a clear log

What you'll find on Odilon:

- Workshops for students to practise the four skills (listening, speaking, reading, and writing) while expanding the theme of each unit

- Vocabulary-building exercises

The interactive activities and material offered by Odilon are only intended for teachers and students using *REAL Skills Book 1* as core material for their course. Registration for Odilon is free. Please note, however, that the support from our customer service staff is only for Canadian users.

Warm-Up

Each unit begins with a different activity to get you **thinking about** and **discussing** each new theme.

To take advantage of a wide range of stimulating workshops and useful material, please visit:

www.cheneliere.ca/esl

Reading

Level-appropriate texts from a variety of sources and text types (newspapers, magazines, etc.) will help you increase your reading skills.

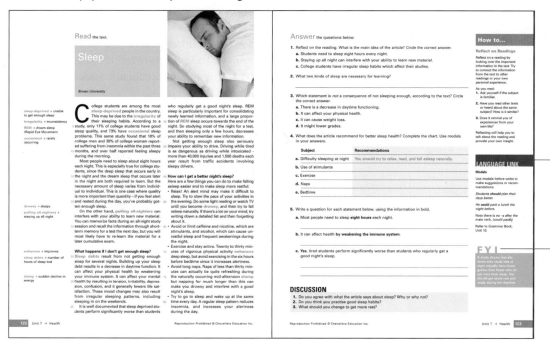

Language Link gives you the language elements and grammar you need to do the required task.

References to *REAL Grammar Book 1* indicate where to get more detailed information and practice.

FYI (For Your Information) provides interesting facts or tips related to the theme.

Listening/Watching

Carefully selected, high-interest audio and video segments include interviews, reports, hip documentaries, and short films. Some units also contain a **language-specific** listening exercise to help build **functional vocabulary** such as numbers, dates, descriptive adjectives, clothing, directions, food items, etc.

Vocabulary

A variety of exercises help you acquire new vocabulary that was carefully selected based on **frequency** and **usefulness**.

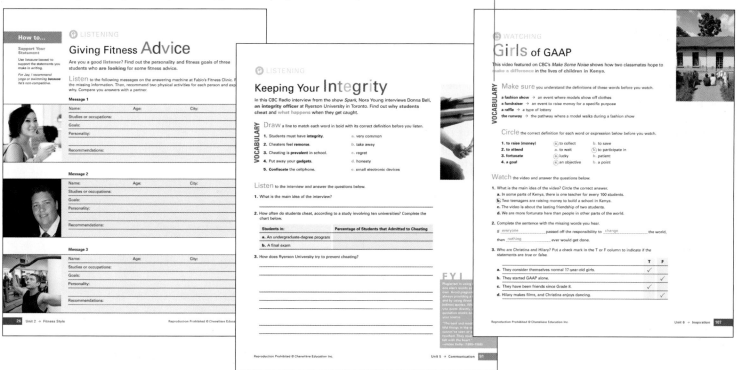

Speaking

Speaking activities offer **real contexts** and range from guided discussions to surveys, creative games to formal presentations.

Numerous **_Discussion_** boxes throughout the unit give you opportunities to get talking and react to various topics.

Integrated **_Pronunciation_** exercises geared to high-beginner to low-intermediate learners help you become a more accurate speaker through guided practice.

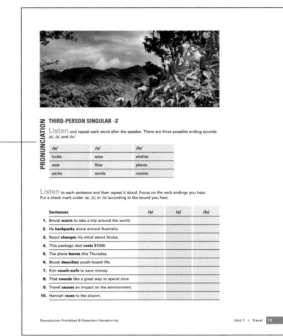

In Words emphasises specific vocabulary building of theme-related words by focusing on elements such as word families, commonly confused or misused words, and functional vocabulary.

How to... helps you acquire useful strategies for your reading, listening, speaking, and writing skills.

Writing Files

Writing Files take you through the writing process **step-by-step**, from writing sentences to paragraphs, and give you examples and hands-on practice of the writing theory.

Integrated into every unit, *Writing Files* reinforce the theme of the unit. However, you can **easily reference** this section on beige pages at any time.

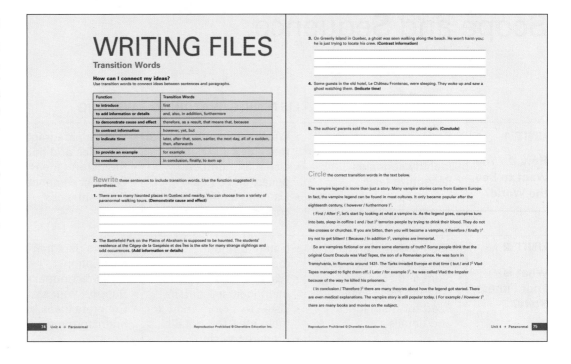

Writing

Integrated writing activities in the units give you practice.

Project Files

Each unit ends with *Project Files* that offer a choice of fun and motivating projects to extend the unit and reinforce the featured language skills.

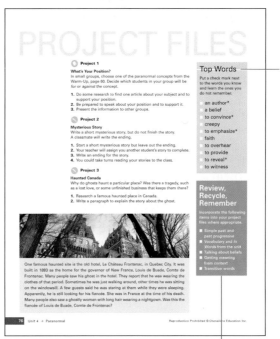

Top Words is a list of 10 vocabulary words featured in the unit, intended to help you reuse and acquire these words. Useful words from the AWL (Academic Word List) are indicated with a star (*) for easy reference.

Review, Recycle, Remember highlights the main focus of the unit and reminds you to integrate these elements into your projects where appropriate.

Scope and Sequence

	READING	LISTENING/WATCHING	WRITING	SPEAKING
UNIT 1 How Do You Want to See the World?	• Read for main ideas and details • Identify cognates • Recognize false cognates	• Watch a documentary for main idea and details • Listen for numbers, prices, and dates • Listen to an interview to compare ways of travel	• Write a paragraph about lifestyles and habits • Brainstorm ideas • Connect sentences • Edit sentences	• Make introductions • Discuss travel options • Interview classmates about lifestyles and habits
UNIT 2 What Is Your Fitness Style?	• Read descriptions and take a personality quiz • Skim and scan • Find the main idea • Read for main ideas and details	• Listen to phone messages • Watch a news report for main idea and details • Listen to a radio show for main idea and details • Prepare to listen	• Write a personal description • Make recommendations • Support your statement • Generate ideas by brainstorming	• Use help strategies • Survey classmates about personality and fitness preferences • Discuss fitness and personality
UNIT 3 Information Evolution	• Read for details • Recognize informal language • Predict events • Read for main ideas and details	• Listen to a radio show for main idea and details • Predict events • Listen for verbs in the simple past • Watch a news report for main idea and details	• Describe a memory • Write paragraphs and topic sentences	• Discuss past and present technology • Discuss technology and manners • Brainstorm and express pros and cons
UNIT 4 Into the Unknown	• Scan for statistics • Read for main ideas and details • Interpret a story and put it in order • Identify the speaker in a text	• Watch an animated video for main idea and details • Listen to an interview for main idea and details	• Write a paragraph about beliefs and explanations • Use transition words	• Complete a survey • Talk about beliefs • Discuss results • Tell a story • Discuss unexplainable events
UNIT 5 Communicate What You Mean	• Highlight essential information • Read to select subtitles for a text • Read for main ideas and details	• Watch a news report for main idea and details • Listen to a conversation for main idea and details • Listen to an interview for main idea and details	• Write a personal profile • Write topic sentences and supporting details	• Discuss lying • Play the lie detector game • Make observations • Talk about perceptions • Avoid overgeneralizations
UNIT 6 What Is Your Inspiration?	• Scan and sort information • Pair read and retell	• Listen to an audio segment to practise question formation • Listen to an interview and and watch a video for main idea and details • Interpret a song	• Write a response letter to agree or disagree • Write a paragraph about future plans • Write a personal motto	• Discuss positive and negative role models • Emphasize your point • Discuss future plans • Ask for clarification
UNIT 7 Examining Health Myths	• Read for main ideas and details • Reflect on readings	• Watch a documentary for main idea and details • Listen for modals in the form of riddles • Listen for directions • Listen to an interview for main idea and details	• Write a riddle using modals • Write advice using modals • Write an opinion paragraph	• Ask and answer health questions • Agree or disagree • Give advice • Give directions • Express an opinion

PRONUNCIATION	VOCABULARY	GRAMMAR	PROJECT FILES
• Third person singular *-s*	• Words and expressions related to travel, nationalities, and countries	• Simple present • Question formation	• Write a travel guide • Write an ad for responsible travel • Produce a travel show
• Contracted forms of the present progressive	• Words and expressions related to fitness and personality • Use *play*, *do* or *go* with fitness words	• Present progressive and gerund form of nouns • Apostrophes	• Write an ad • Present a radio broadcast • Write a blog
• The *-ed* ending of regular past tense verbs	• Words and expressions related to technology • Choose the correct definition in a dictionary	• Simple past • Past questions • Past expressions	• Write about the impact of technology • Present a past event using pictures • Present the evolution of technology
• Words with silent letters	• Words and expressions related to the paranormal • Word families • Get meaning from context	• Past progressive • Review of simple past • Possessive *-s*	• Support and present your position *for* or *against* • Finish a story • Research and write a paragraph
• Words spelled with *ei*	• Words and expressions related to communication • Body parts and their movements • Physical description words	• Comparatives with *worse, the worst, as bad as* • Comparisons with *than* • Superlatives	• Prepare and carry out a questionnaire • Write a personal ad • Play the citizenship game
• Words that begin with *h-*	• Words and expressions related to inspiration • Clothing vocabulary	• Future with *will* and *be going to* • Adverbs • Uncountable nouns	• Write a paragraph about a role model • Research and present song lyrics • Interview someone admirable
• The /th/ sound • *Can* vs. *can't*	• Words and expressions related to health • Expressions using the verb *get*	• Modals • Plural nouns • Countable and uncountable nouns	• Write about a personal experience • Present environmentally friendly options • Research and write about health myths

Table of Contents

How Do You Want to See the
WORLD?

Latest trends give travellers more OPTIONS

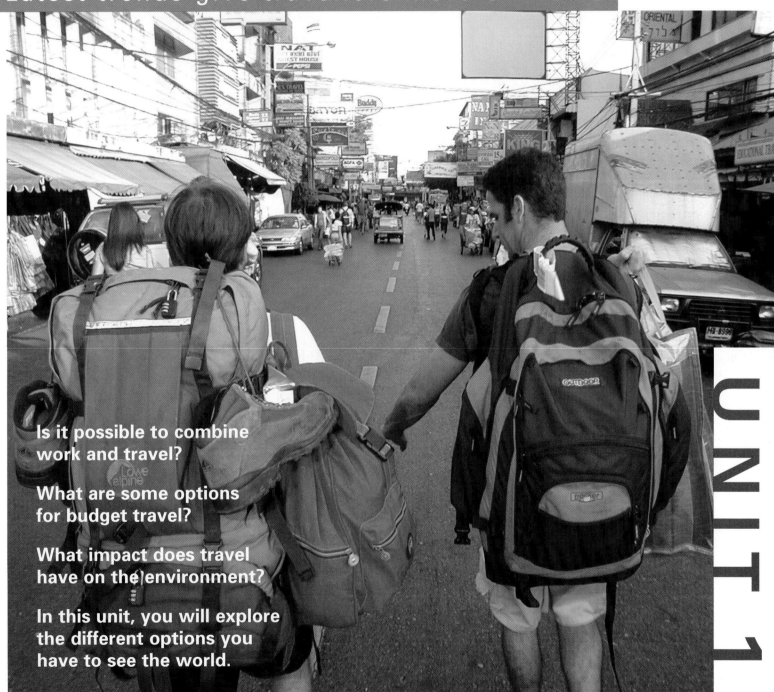

Is it possible to combine work and travel?

What are some options for budget travel?

What impact does travel have on the environment?

In this unit, you will explore the different options you have to see the world.

UNIT 1

ON THE GO!

 WARM-UP

Language Exchange

People travel for many reasons: to work, to relax, even to **learn English**. English is spoken in many different **countries** as a first or second language. English contains many words from other languages, like **French** and Spanish.

Look at the words below and guess which language they come from. Fill in the missing letters to complete the name of each language and the name of a country where that language is spoken.

	English Word	Language of Origin	A Country Where Spoken
1.	Opera	I ___ a ___ ian	I ___ a ___ y
2.	Kindergarten	___ erman	Germa ___ ___
3.	Guitar	Spanish	Sp ___ ___ n
4.	Athlete	Greek	Gre ___ ___ e
5.	Dracula	R ___ ma ___ i ___ n	Roman ___ ___
6.	Alcohol	Ar ___ bi ___	E ___ y ___ t
7.	Yacht	D ___ t ___ h	Netherlands
8.	Futon	___ apa ___ es ___	Jap ___ ___
9.	Sauna	F ___ nni ___ ___	Finland
10.	Ballet	Fr ___ ___ ch	Fr ___ ___ ce

How to...

Make Introductions

To introduce yourself:
Hi, my name is Sophia.
Hi, I'm Sam.
Let me introduce myself.

To introduce someone else:
This is Valerie.
Let me introduce you to Eric.

Responses:
Nice to meet you.
Pleased to meet you.

LANGUAGE LINK

Simple Present

Use the simple present to talk about facts, habits, and preferences.

Make sure to add -s or -es to regular verbs in the third-person singular (*he, she,* or *it*)

Refer to Grammar Book, Unit 1.

DISCUSSION

1. Do you speak any of the languages from the list? Which ones?
2. Which cities or countries do you want to visit? Why?

Introduce your partner to another team. Include the information from the discussion and use How to... as a guide. Use the simple present tense in your introduction.

*This **is** Frederic. He **speaks** French and Spanish. He **wants** to visit British Columbia because he **loves** to ski. He also **hopes** to practise English.*

READING

Sail Away!

How do you combine a career and travel? You can work on a **cruise ship**! In this interview, Inga, a cruise-ship employee discusses what life is like at sea.

FYI

Today more than a billion people all over the world speak English. There are so many reasons to learn English. It is the language that unites business people and travellers all over the world. It is also the main language of the Internet. Why do you want to learn English?

VOCABULARY

Match each word or expression with its correct definition before you read. The line number is in parentheses.

1. a manager (3)	a. nice, attractive
2. to hire (4)	b. suggestions for help
3. to spend (17)	c. to use time
4. advice (21)	d. to give someone a job
5. to deal with (22)	e. a supervisor
6. pretty (33)	f. to care
7. to mind (61)	g. to fix a problem
8. skills (65)	h. abilities

Read the first and second paragraphs, and notice the cognates in bold. Find and underline ten different cognates in the seventh paragraph. As you read, focus on the cognates to help you understand the text better.

Read the interview and fill in the missing question words.

what	why	who	do	where

Life on a Cruise Ship

An Interview with Inga

1. Q: _____ do you do?
A: I work on a cruise ship as a **human resources** and training manager. I train new people that the cruise ship hires. I also work
5 closely with the crew and the **captain**. I usually work for four months at a time and go home for two months on **vacation**.

2. Q: _____ do you work on a cruise ship?
A: I work on a ship because I love the **ocean**
10 and I enjoy **visiting** a new **island** or **port** every day. I don't like **routine** chores. On a ship, I don't shop for groceries, do laundry, or cook. There are many **restaurants** where we can eat good food whenever we want.

How to...

Identify Cognates

Sometimes an English word looks like a word in another language and has a similar meaning. These words are cognates. About one third of English words come from French. Sometimes there are only minor differences in the spelling.

When you identify cognates, you can understand parts of a text without using a dictionary.

crew → employees on a ship

chores → housework

Couch-Surfing Anyone?

Whether you travel for one year or one week, a vacation is **expensive**. A popular trend called couch-surfing helps **budget travellers** save money.

VOCABULARY

Match each word or expression with its correct definition before you read. The line number is in parentheses.

1. The **guest** is late. (2)		**a.** people we do not know
2. They are **strangers**. (3)		**b.** sofa
3. She sleeps on the **couch**. (8)		**c.** extra
4. Do you have a **spare** room? (9)		**d.** not expensive
5. This is very **cheap**. (43)		**e.** visitor
6. There are many **locals** at this place. (46)		**f.** residents of a place
7. We don't **do laundry**. (77)		**g.** person who receives guests
8. Where is the **host**? (80)		**h.** wash clothes

Read the text.

Montrealer Started Couchsurfing

Learn about the newest class of travellers

By Jasmin Legotas
Montreal Gazette

founded → started

There we were, three Canadian girls, about to spend five days as guests of Sebastien Bernier, a complete stranger. What were we thinking?

5 We were doing what thousands of people around the world have started to do: we were going couch-surfing.

A website lets people offer their couch, spare bedroom, floor-space or backyard to 10 other people visiting their part of the world. Or, if they have no spare room, they can offer to meet you for a coffee or drink and show you around their town.

Like many social networking websites, 15 couch-surfing is free and anyone can join. The website now has more than 100,000 members spread across every continent in more than 200 countries. It touches many languages, cultures and religions. North America and Europe have 20 the most couch-surfers.

The average age of couch-surfers is 27, but even people over 80 go couch-surfing! Many people in their 50s are members. Montreal has 2,100 members—more than any other city in 25 the world. It is also the first and only city with a couch-surfing office.

Montreal surfer Mathieu Groulx had visited the Big Apple before, but surfing "felt like I was arriving at an old friend's," he said. "Going as a 30 couch-surfer was a very different experience than in past trips. You get to see places you might never know about if you stayed in a hotel or hostel," he added.

Casey Fenton from Maine, **founded** Couch 35 Surfing.com as a simple accommodation exchange. But as its popularity grew, so did its features: online chat, bulletin boards, interest groups, city meet-ups, verifications and newsletters.

40 The idea behind couch-surfing, Fenton says, is to help people "create adventures they will remember." The original couch-surfer, Fenton got the idea by chance. He got some cheap tickets to Iceland but deplored the idea of staying in 45 a hostel. He wanted the real taste of Reykjavik; the one only locals truly experience.

Fenton emailed 1,500 students at the University of Reykjavik, asking if anyone would be willing to host him in their city. It worked: 50 between 50 and 100 replied, "yeah, come surf my couch." Fenton then started the Couch Surfing website. Even his dad does it. "It's like immediately becoming a citizen of a place," Mark Fenton says.

55 Giancarlo Russo, an Italian native living in Wales, has surfed more than 20 couches in the past year. "Couch-surfing is a lovely thing," said Russo. "When you surf with someone, you share a bit of your life; you move a step farther 60 than sharing a house."

"It's a good chance to explore, to meet other

people who really like to travel and to meet people around the world," he added.

On the grand scale of life, couch-surfing is 65 about creating a world without discrimination, Groulx said.

For many couch-surfers, it's the late-night conversations with a stranger, the all-night partying with a new friend or the discovery that they're 70 the only tourist at a neighbourhood **hangout** that creates long-lasting memories.

With couch-surfing, however, you take what you get—there's no complaining to the concierge.

75 At the apartment in Paris where my friends and I spent five nights, we had free wireless Internet, an offer to do our laundry, a beautiful view and a central location.

At our next surf in Rome, we spent three days 80 sharing our host's tiny living room with many musical instruments and bookshelves. In Florence, I had my own bed—and bed bugs— and in **Pistoia**, my host welcomed me into his home on a day's notice with a pasta dinner and 85 homemade wine.

hangout → a place where friends often meet

Pistoia → a city in Italy

Answer the questions below.

1. What is the purpose of the CouchSurfing website?
   a. It is a free, social networking site.
   b. It connects people with travellers who plan to sleep on their couch.
   c. It allows people to meet the locals while travelling.
   d. All of the above are correct.

2. What age are the people who couch-surf?
   a. People under age 27 go couch-surfing.
   b. People of all ages go couch-surfing.
   c. Only people between ages 27 and 80 go couch-surfing.

3. How does Mathieu Groulx describe his experience as a couch-surfer?
   a. He saw the Big Apple for the first time.
   b. He stayed at an old friend's house.
   c. He said you get to see places you don't normally see otherwise.
   d. He said it was like past trips.

4. What do we know about Casey Fenton? Put a check mark in the T or F column to indicate if the statement is *true* or *false*.

	T	F
a. He hoped to stay at a hostel in Iceland.		
b. He wanted to see Iceland the way the local people did.		
c. He asked university students to host him.		
d. Only a few students invited him to stay with them.		

Responsible Tourism

More and more people are trying to reduce the impact that travel has on **local people** and the environment. **Ecotourism** and **sustainable travel** are two responsible travel options to consider. This interview gives us tips on how to take a **low-impact trip.**

VOCABULARY

Circle the correct definition for each word or expression before you listen.

1. a much-needed **income**	**a.** visit	**b.** salary
2. to involve yourself	**a.** include	**b.** invite
3. to earn money	**a.** lose	**b.** make
4. fair price	**a.** reasonable	**b.** high
5. to go **on foot**	**a.** without shoes	**b.** by walking

Listen to the interview and then answer the questions below.

1. Complete the sentence by writing the missing words you hear.

If you are someone who loves _____ and learning _____ things, then

responsible _____ is for you.

2. Compare a responsible tourist with a regular tourist by completing the chart below.

Aspects of Travel	Responsible Tourist	Regular Tourist
a. Local culture		
b. Tours		
c. Size of travel groups		
d. Transportation		

3. "There are so many ways to make vacations fun without flying," says Vera Sims. With a partner, brainstorm two ideas for a weekend getaway in your city or town.

DISCUSSION

1. Do you think that travel harms the environment? Why or why not?
2. Do you want to change the way you travel? Why or why not?
3. What else can we do to reduce our impact?

WRITING FILES

Sentence Structure

What is a sentence?

A sentence should be complete and able to stand alone. It contains a subject and a verb.
It can be:

A statement: *Couch-surfing is free to join.*

A question: *Does Brook meet many people in Australia?*

A command: *Think about your impact when you travel.*

An exclamation: *We have to share our room at the hostel with eight other people!*

Read the sentences below. Circle C or I to indicate if the statement is *complete* or *incomplete*.
If it is *incomplete*, write the correct statement on the line provided.

1. Because she likes to travel.   **C   I**

_____

2. And a responsible traveller, too.   **C   I**

_____

3. Couch-surfing requires some trust   **C   I**

_____

4. And now, all about life in a youth hostel.   **C   I**

_____

5. The people Brook meets as he travels around the world.   **C   I**

_____

How do I edit sentences?

Make sure your sentences are grammatically correct. Use the checklist to help you identify errors.

1. ☐ Is there a subject and a verb?

2. ☐ Are the verb tenses correct?

3. ☐ If necessary, does the sentence include *do* or *does* for questions and negative forms?

4. ☐ Is the first word of each sentence capitalized?
     Have you put a capital on other words that require one?

5. ☐ Is there a period or other punctuation mark at the end of your sentence?
     Are the apostrophes in the correct place?

Edit these sentences by crossing out the mistake and writing the correction on the line provided. Use the checklist to verify your sentences.

1. i love couch-surfing but my friend does'nt.

_____

_____

2. We want to visit antarctica in July.

_____

_____

3. you want to go couch-surfing with me?

_____

_____

4. They not responsible tourists.

_____

_____

5. Its really beautiful on the island of st Vincent.

_____

_____

How do I combine sentences?

Sometimes, two short sentences can be written as one sentence. You can join sentences by using connecting words.

Use _or, and_ or _but_ to connect the information in the following sentence pairs.

1. She could go on a cruise ship. She could take a responsible tourism trip. **(or)**

_____

_____

_____

2. I have to check my emails. I have to organize Crew Karaoke for tonight. **(and)**

_____

_____

_____

3. They don't like couch-surfing. They think it is better for students to couch-surf. **(but)**

_____

_____

_____

4. Go to the visitors' centre. Find out more about the local culture. **(and)**

_____

_____

_____

PROJECT FILES

 Project 1

A Travel Guide

You are a travel writer for a travel magazine! Describe a city or country of your choice. List the top five activities for this destination.

1. Choose a destination and find information on it.
2. Describe the top five activities.
3. Use visual support (pictures, posters, etc.).

  Project 2

A Package Tour

In teams, make an ad for a responsible travel tour of your choice.

1. Find information on responsible travel or ecotourism.
2. Create your own slogan, write a logo, and describe the mission or purpose of your travel tour and what makes it responsible.
3. Write the name of the destination, its location, cost of the tour, and contact information (address, phone number, email address, website, etc.).
4. Describe the important aspects of the tour.
5. Include what to do and what not to do on the tour.

 Project 3

The Travel Show

In teams, produce a live TV show for the top five things to see in a city or town near you. Choose a different aspect of tourism in your city or town to present from the list below:

Night life	Shopping	Cultural or outdoor activities
Markets	Fine dining	Fast food
Other points of interest		

Top Words

Put a check mark next to the words you know and learn the ones you do not remember.

- ☐ advice
- ☐ cheap
- ☐ a guest
- ☐ to involve* yourself
- ☐ a local
- ☐ to spend
- ☐ to travel
- ☐ a trip
- ☐ a vacancy
- ☐ a vacation

Review, Recycle, Remember

Incorporate the following items into your project files where appropriate.

- ■ Simple present
- ■ Vocabulary and *In Words* related to travel
- ■ Making introductions
- ■ Identifying cognates
- ■ Recognizing false cognates
- ■ Sentence structure

What Is Your Fitness
STYLE?

How personality affects the choices we make about FITNESS

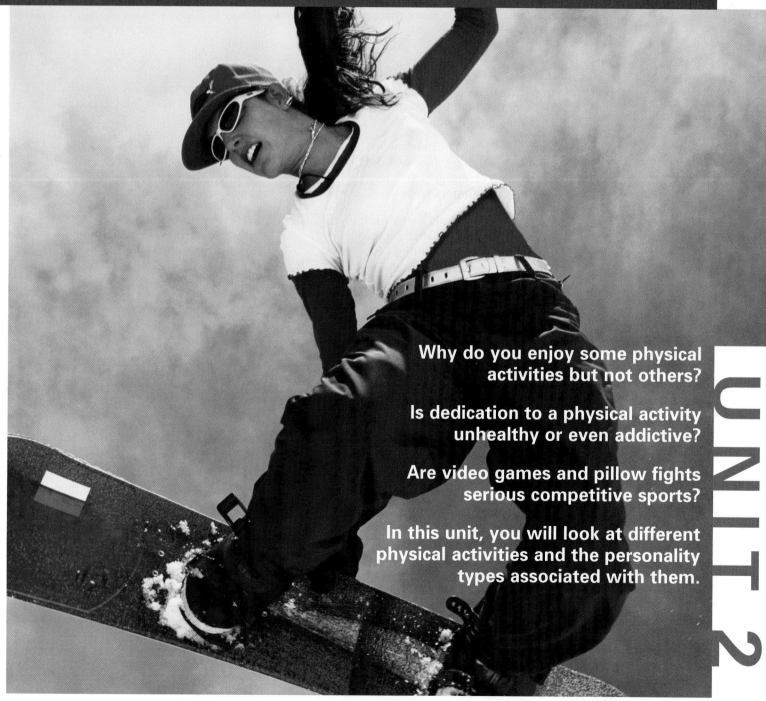

Why do you enjoy some physical activities but not others?

Is dedication to a physical activity unhealthy or even addictive?

Are video games and pillow fights serious competitive sports?

In this unit, you will look at different physical activities and the personality types associated with them.

UNIT 2

ARE YOU GAME?

ⓣ WARM-UP

Test Your Personality

Are you obsessed with **competition**? Do you usually avoid taking risks? A Montreal researcher, Dr. James Gavin, discovered a connection between **fitness choices** and **personality**. Take the quiz to find out more about your personality.

How to...

Use Help Strategies

To ask how to say something in English:
How do you say _____ in English?

To ask how to spell a word:
How do you spell _____?

To ask what a word means:
What does _____ mean?

to interact → to socialize with other people

willpower → the ability to control yourself

task → a job you must do

better safe than sorry → better to be careful than to take risks

Read the descriptions for each personality trait. Select the one that best describes your personality by putting a check mark in the appropriate box.

← **More like this**   **More like this** →

Social ☐ ☐ ☐ ☐ ☐ **Non-social**
I love to be with people, to interact, and to do things in groups. I don't enjoy doing things by myself. | I prefer doing things alone. I enjoy solitude. I find social interactions tiring.

Spontaneous ☐ ☐ ☐ ☐ ☐ **Controlled**
I enjoy doing things without planning in advance. Routines bore me. | I like to plan and feel in control. I want to know what will happen next. I enjoy routines. I don't like surprises.

Internally motivated ☐ ☐ ☐ ☐ ☐ **Externally motivated**
I'm 100% self-motivated. I have exceptionally strong willpower. I don't rely on others for support. | I need support to do difficult things. Rewards and social encouragement help me to stay committed.

Competitive ☐ ☐ ☐ ☐ ☐ **Non-competitive**
I enjoy competitive games. I perform better when I compete. Competition is fun. | I avoid competitive situations. Competition makes me feel uncomfortable. If I have to compete, I don't perform well.

Aggressive ☐ ☐ ☐ ☐ ☐ **Non-aggressive**
I'm a forceful, assertive person. I take action. I won't let things get in my way. I make sure my needs are met. | I'm easygoing and relaxed, maybe even passive about meeting my needs. I dislike aggression and avoid confrontation.

Focused ☐ ☐ ☐ ☐ ☐ **Unfocused**
It's easy for me to concentrate and stay focused on tasks. I enjoy absorbing myself in what I'm doing. | I'm easily distracted. I have difficulty focusing on one task. I prefer doing lots of different things at the same time.

Risk-seeking ☐ ☐ ☐ ☐ ☐ **Risk-avoiding**
I'm a thrill-seeker. I love adventure. I'm willing to take big risks to do the things that appeal to me. | I avoid risks. I say "better safe than sorry," even if it means not doing something that appeals to me. I'm a careful person.

Write a short description of yourself based on your quiz results. Then discuss your personality type with a partner.

_____

_____

 READING

Tai Chi or Basketball?

Now that you know more about your **personality type**, learn about Dr. Gavin's research. He offers advice on matching **physical activities** to personality types.

Circle the correct definition of the word in bold before you read the text.

1. He **creates** fitness programs for you.
   a. makes   **b.** gives

2. I **stick** to an exercise routine.
   a. avoid   **b.** commit

3. There are **fewer** distractions.
   a. not as many   **b.** many

4. **Risk-taking** sports include mountain biking and downhill skiing.
   a. safe   **b.** dangerous

5. Swimming **suits** you.
   a. goes well with   **b.** challenges

6. All sports have different **demands**.
   a. equipment   **b.** requirements

7. This physical activity is a good **match** for you.
   a. fit   **b.** competition

8. The university researcher **trains** lifestyle coaches.
   a. hires   **b.** teaches

Read the article.

Researcher Finds Sports that Fit Each Personality

By Kristian Peltonen
National Post

A Montreal researcher has created a model to help those who can't stick to an exercise routine find physical activities that match their personality.

5 Someone who has trouble focusing on one task, for example, should probably put the squash racquet away and stick to something with fewer distractions, like jogging or swimming.

Someone who enjoys being around other 10 people will be more likely to keep exercising if they choose team sports over yoga, for example.

James Gavin, 62, of the Centre of Applied Human Sciences at Concordia University, created the model by finding seven "personal styles" 15 from studies on personality in sports: sociability, spontaneity, self-motivation, aggressiveness, competitiveness, mental focus, and risk-taking.

Basketball, for example, requires social inter- action and competitive energy, but running on a 20 **treadmill** does not, he said.

"All physical activities have different psych- ological demands of participants," he said. "These demands may match or **mismatch** an individual's personal style."

25 Gavin's research found a "significant trend" between the amount people exercise and the degree to which their activities match their personalities.

He now trains lifestyle fitness coaches to use 30 the model to help people find what activities suit their personality best.

The model can also be used through **self- administered tests**, such as one he developed that uses a computer questionnaire, much like 35 vocational guidance tools.

But some people "will profit from talking with a professional," he said.

More dedicated individuals can take the model further, said Gavin. By choosing activ- 40 ities that go against their personality, people can make their own personality more like that of the activity they choose.

Taking up running, for example, can help bring out your competitive side, he said. 45 Switching from a sport like racquetball to tai chi can help reduce aggression.

treadmill → walking machine used for exercise

mismatch → a bad fit

self-administered tests → tests you take by yourself

taking up → start doing

Write your answers to these questions in the first column of the chart below.

1. Which physical activity do you participate in the most?

2. What personality traits are associated with this physical activity? To find out, refer to page 23 and look at the position of the physical activity in each column. For example, downhill skiing is risk-seeking behaviour, and tai chi is risk-avoiding behaviour.

3. Is this physical activity a good match for your personality type? Refer to your results from the personality-type quiz on page 20. Is it a good match? Why or why not?

4. If it is not a good match, what physical activities would better match your personality?

Survey two other classmates and complete the chart below.

	You	Student 1	Student 2
1. Physical activity			
2. Personality traits			
3. Personality match?	☐ Yes ☐ No	☐ Yes ☐ No	☐ Yes ☐ No
4. Suggestions for a better match (if necessary)			

IN WORDS

Play, Do, or Go?
We use the verbs *play*, *do*, or *go* to talk about physical activities. But do you know which verb goes with which physical activity? It all depends on the kind of activity it is.

Use the verb **play** before the name of a competitive team sport.

*He **is playing** hockey this season.*

Use the verb **do** before the name of a group sport.

*They **do** karate on the weekend.*

Use the verb **go** before the name of a physical activity you can usually do alone, and that ends in *-ing*.

*She **is going** hiking this weekend.*

Note: Use the verb **practise** to talk about training.

*I **practise** gymnastics twice a week.*

Complete the sentences below by filling in the blanks with *play*, *do*, or *go*. Use the correct form of the verb in your answers (simple present or present progressive). Pay attention to negative forms.

1. They _____ baseball right now.

2. I _____ skiing every weekend.

3. She _____ aerobics at the moment.

4. They (not) _____ soccer this semester.

5. We _____ tai chi every morning.

6. Right now, he _____ martial arts.

7. The class (not) _____ hiking now.

8. I (not) _____ tennis often.

9. Look at how the teacher _____ yoga.

10. The students _____ volleyball on Wednesdays.

PRONUNCIATION

CONTRACTED FORMS OF THE PRESENT PROGRESSIVE

Listen to the long forms and the contracted forms of the present progressive. Repeat each sentence aloud.

	Long Form	Contraction	Negative Long Form	Negative Contraction
1.	I am running.	I'm running.	I am not running.	I'm not running.
2.	You are training.	You're training.	You are not training.	You're not training.
3.	He is canoeing.	He's canoeing.	He is not canoeing.	He's not canoeing.
4.	She is skating.	She's skating.	She is not skating.	She's not skating.
5.	We are boxing.	We're boxing.	We are not boxing.	We're not boxing.
6.	They are dancing.	They're dancing.	They are not dancing.	They're not dancing.

Listen to the statements below and fill in the blanks with the contracted form you hear. Pay attention to the position of the apostrophe.

1. He _____ with his family in the Adirondack Mountains.

2. She _____ .

3. It _____ too hard for the race.

4. They _____ there for their turn.

5. This is where we _____ tennis.

6. I _____ yoga right now.

7. You _____ on your technique.

8. John _____ on the hockey team this year.

9. Sue _____ tai chi for the first time.

10. Take its toy away; it _____ the dogsled right now.

LANGUAGE LINK

Using an Apostrophe

An apostrophe replaces a letter, or letters, in the contracted form of a word.

Write the apostrophe in the same place as the letter you removed.

He is training hard.

He's training for a competition.

Giving Fitness Advice

Are you a good **listener**? Find out the personality and fitness goals of three students who **are looking** for some fitness advice.

Listen to the following messages on the answering machine at Fabio's Fitness Clinic. Fill in the missing information. Then, recommend two physical activities for each person and explain why. Compare you answers with a partner.

Message 1

Name:	Age:	City:

Studies or occupations:

Goals:

Personality:

Recommendations:

Message 2

Name:	Age:	City:

Studies or occupations:

Goals:

Personality:

Recommendations:

Message 3

Name:	Age:	City:

Studies or occupations:

Goals:

Personality:

Recommendations:

READING

A Sports Addict Confesses

In his personal blog, Brad describes his **love of sports**. He is quite athletic, maybe too much so! Decide if you think Brad has an **addictive personality**.

FYI

Do genes influence people's personalities, including a preference for certain sports? Some scientists think so. Brain chemistry could make someone more likely to do a dangerous sport. People who seek thrills and excitement by doing extreme sports, like ice-wall climbing or riding a BMX bicycle, could have a gene for adventure!

VOCABULARY

Draw a line to match each word or expression in bold with its correct definition before you read. The line number is in parentheses.

1. **to struggle** (24)
2. **to drop** (39)
3. **to squeeze in** (39)
4. **to reduce** (47)
5. **neglect** (54)

a. to barely make time for
b. to make smaller or less
c. to stop doing an activity
d. lack of care
e. to have difficulty doing something

Read the blog.

My Name Is Brad, and I Am Addicted to Sports

By Brad Culp

My friends and family repeatedly tell me that I'm addicted to sports. I spend up to 30 hours each week swimming, biking, and running around like a little kid. I also spend time playing collegiate water polo, and I will try rowing this fall. I also began cyclocross and ultra-marathoning this year, just to pass the time.

So, yes, I have a bit of an addictive personality. But I can think of worse things to be addicted to than sports. Even in my own life, many people I know develop bad habits. I have a brother who is addicted to fast food and a father addicted to his BlackBerry. My girlfriend needs to watch bad television programming every single day.

When you have an addiction, you have to know when to take it easy. This is the key to staying healthy. **Fracturing** my foot this April reminded me that it was time to **cut back**. Trying to complete an ultra-marathon and Ironman in the same month is about as intelligent as bathing with your toaster.

After struggling to finish an Ironman triathlon last weekend, I decided that I need a break in order to make it through the season. I went back to my hometown with plans to spend more time with a beer in my hand than a sports drink. I left my bike, my running shoes, and my **goggles** behind.

It was definitely a refreshing change. For the first time in ages, I spent more time with loved ones than with my much-loved bike. I was able to really enjoy sleeping in on a Saturday morning instead of drinking too much coffee and then taking a long bike ride. My daily hours of

fracturing → breaking
cut back → do less often

goggles → safety glasses, often used in sports

sleep and containers of Ben and Jerry's ice cream doubled, and my hours of training dropped. I only had one impulse to squeeze in
40 a workout. While enjoying a few drinks on a lakeside beach, I wanted to take a little swim around the lake. My friends quickly reminded me that the swim was a few kilometres long, happy hour was about to start, and that I need-
45 ed professional help.

While I enjoyed the break, it did little to reduce my addiction. I lived a completely op- posite lifestyle for a week, and now I'm ready to go back to normal. If anything, the brief break
50 from doing all my sports made the addiction get worse. I returned to my apartment late last night to find my running shoes waiting by the door for me, and they were looking lonely after a week of neglect. I tried to resist them, but it
55 was no use. I laced up my running shoes and started jogging. I don't think I'm going to **kick this habit** any time soon. I would need a lot more than a **12-step program**.

kick this habit → stop doing this habit

12-step program → the 12 stages used to help people beat addictions

Answer the questions below.

1. What is Brad's personality type? Provide examples from the text to support your answer.

_____

_____

2. Which activities does Brad participate in? Circle all the correct answers.

    a. swimming   **c.** water polo   **e.** rowing   **g.** horseback riding

    b. biking   **d.** yoga   **f.** ultra-marathoning

3. What forced Brad to cut back on sports? Circle the correct answer.

    a. He realized that he has an addiction.

    b. He injured himself by fracturing his foot.

    c. His friends and family told him that he needed help.

4. How did Brad's habits change during his break from physical activities?

_____

_____

5. What three things did Brad's friends remind him of when he wanted to take a little swim around the lake? Circle all the correct answers.

    a. It was a long swim around the lake.   **c.** Happy hour was about to start.

    b. He promised to take a break from sports.   **d.** He needed professional help.

6. After Brad took a break from sports, did his addiction lessen, get worse, or stay the same? Support your answer.

_____

_____

DISCUSSION

    1. Do you think Brad has an addiction? Why or why not?

    2. When does dedication to an activity become unhealthy?

Game Whiz

Ryan Ward is training to defend his title as a world champion. Is **gaming** an addiction, a professional, competitive sport, or even a **career**? This CBC News: *Sunday* report features a young man who is doing what many teenagers only **dream** about.

VOCABULARY

Make sure you understand the definitions of the words in bold before you watch.

to apply → to register for courses

gamers → people who play video games

gaming → sport of playing video games

to knock out → to eliminate

mainstream → common; played by many people

over the hill → too old

to peak → to be at its highest point

to put a lot into it → to make a big effort

Watch the video, and then answer the questions below.

1. Circle T or F to indicate if the statement below is *true* or *false*. If it is *false*, write the correct statement on the line provided.

a. Ryan Ward is 18 years old.   T   F

_____

b. Ryan has turned gaming into a career.   T   F

_____

c. Ryan has made about $55,000 this year playing video games.   T   F

_____

2. What game is Ryan Ward training for?

_____

3. When Ryan was growing up, what did his mother say about video games?

_____

_____

4. How much money does Ryan make a year playing video games in his gaming league?

_____

_____

5. Who are most of the competitors at the World Cyber Games, and how old are they?

_____

_____

6. How do the competitors win in Ryan's video game event?

_____

_____

7. What are five countries that Ryan competes against at the World Cyber Games?

_____

_____

8. Did Ryan lose at the World Cyber Games because he was too old? Explain.

_____

_____

DISCUSSION

1. Is playing video games an acceptable competitive sport?
2. What are the qualities of a good gamer?
3. Ryan quit his job and did not enter university. Is he wasting his time choosing a career that only lasts for about five years?

READING

Ultimate Fun

Are you a very **social person**? Are you competitive but enjoy playing with strong team spirit? If so, a game called **Ultimate** may just be the perfect game for you.

Circle the correct definition of each word and expression below before you read. The line number is in parentheses.

1. to be hooked (14)   **a.** addicted   **b.** curved

2. to boom (16)   **a.** to decrease   **b.** to become popular

3. to handle (27)   **a.** to manipulate   **b.** to hang on to

4. to settle (31)   **a.** to resolve a problem   **b.** to avoid a problem

Skim the text quickly and put a check mark next to the important topics that are mentioned.

1. The history of Ultimate ☐

2. How to play Ultimate ☐

3. How much it costs to play Ultimate ☐

4. People who enjoy playing Ultimate ☐

Scan the text quickly to find this information.

1. The year Ultimate was started: _____

2. The number of members in Montreal: _____

3. The number of teams in Montreal: _____

4. Where Ultimate was started: _____

5. How many times a week Mike Kropveld plays: _____

Ultimately, It's About Having Fun

By Jill Barker
Montreal Gazette

When Joanne Minns moved to Montreal a few years ago, she found a unique way to meet people.

5 "I posted my name on the bulletin board of the Montreal Ultimate Association," she said.

She made new friends, and found herself addicted to a new sport. "I play three or four times a week in the summer and once or twice a 10 week in the winter," she said. Talk to any Ultimate player and they will tell you how quickly the sport becomes an addiction.

"Once you throw a perfect disc, you're hooked," said Toby Goodfellow, a three-year 15 **veteran** of the game.

Ultimate is booming in Montreal. With 1,700 members playing in its summer and winter (indoor) leagues, the league's 90 teams now **occupy** 10 fields spread across the city and a 20 select number of indoor sites in the winter. Not bad for a game that was started in 1968 by a **nerdy** bunch of New Jersey kids.

Originally called Frisbee Football, the game is a fast-paced non-contact sport that demands 25 speed, agility, and the ability to throw a disc with precision.

"Handling the disc is not like handling a ball," Goodfellow said.

Even though Ultimate is very competitive, 30 there are no referees. Instead, the sport **relies on decorum** and mutual respect to settle any disputes.

"It's about fun, fair play, and trusting the other person," Minns said.

35 Goodfellow said novice players sometimes have difficulty playing a sport without referees. But the spirit of the game is more important than making the right moves. Spirit points are awarded to teams who keep the game fun and respect 40 their opponents. Cheers before and after the game are encouraged. Players often sing songs or play in **goofy** clothing, a difference from most sports where winning is more important than how the game is played.

45 Mike Kropveld, 55, has been playing Ultimate for 12 years, a reminder to Minns that the game is for all ages. Kropveld says he plays three times a week, all year round. "Wherever I go, I have a disc in my car."

50 "The mature players are sometimes the best players—and that's encouraging," said Minns. She also likes the fact that Ultimate is a **coed** sport, normally with four men and three women on a team, which means she can share her love 55 of the sport with her boyfriend, who also plays on the team. Minns says it's a great way to meet members of the opposite sex.

"It's not a singles group, but many members have ended up finding their partner through 60 Ultimate," she said.

Kropveld also likes the coed aspect of the game. He's played on a lot of different teams with players of all ages, and he always manages to have a great time—so much so that he can't 65 imagine life without Ultimate.

"I don't see myself stopping anytime soon," he said. "I'm in good shape and my speed is good. The question is: What's going to happen when I don't play?"

goofy → strange, silly

veteran → experienced person

coed → mixed males and females

occupy → take up space

nerdy → not popular or cool

relies on → depends on, needs

decorum → good manners, politeness

Read the text again and answer the questions below.

1. What is the main idea of the article? Circle the correct answer.

    a. Ultimate becomes an addiction quickly.

    b. Ultimate is a fast-paced, non-contact sport.

    c. Many people enjoy playing Ultimate, a game which is different from most sports.

    d. It is important to have fun.

2. How did Joanne Minns meet new people in Montreal? Write your answer below.

_____

_____

3. How do we know that Ultimate is booming in Montreal? Use your own words to explain.

_____

_____

_____

4. What are the qualities a player needs to play Ultimate? Circle the correct answer.

    a. There are no rules. Anyone who is social can play.

    b. A player needs to have agility, speed, and precision.

    c. A person needs to have an aggressive and competitive personality.

5. Which statement about Ultimate is *true*? Circle the correct answer.

    a. Winning is the most important thing.

    b. There are no referees.

    c. Ultimate was started in 1969 in New Jersey.

    d. The best players are the new players.

6. Put a check mark in the T column to indicate if the statement is *true*.

Ultimate Player	Statement 1	T	Statement 2	T
a. Joanne Minns	Ultimate is a singles group.		It's a great place to meet members of the opposite sex.	
b. Toby Goodfellow	Playing Ultimate is addictive.		Handling a disc is like handling a ball.	
c. Mike Kropveld	I like playing with both men and women on a team.		I do not see myself stopping Ultimate anytime soon.	

7. How is Ultimate different from other competitive team sports, like volleyball or football? Write three examples below.

_____

_____

_____

🎧 LISTENING

Flying Feathers

If you are competitive but **not very athletic**, what physical activity would be right for you? Listen to this **true story** from CBC *Outfront* about a girl who finally figured out the answer for herself.

Make sure you understand the definitions of the words below before you listen.

to choke → to squeeze someone's throat
to glare → to look at with anger
to rehash → to bring up a subject again
to smother → to cover someone's face so the person cannot breathe
to surrender → to give up
a weapon → an instrument of defense

Listen to Amanda's personal story and answer the questions below.

1. What is Amanda studying at Ryerson University? What other subjects interest her?

_____

_____

_____

2. How old is she?

_____

3. What is Amanda's "tragic adolescent story"?

_____

_____

_____

How to...

Prepare to Listen

Before you listen:

1. Read the title, questions, and any other information about the listening segment.

2. Learn any new vocabulary to help you understand better.

3. Try to predict what the listening segment will be about.

4. Be ready to take notes about the key points.

4. Why does Amanda pillow fight now that she is a student at university? Circle all the statements that are true.

   a. She finally found a sport she could win.

   b. She likes getting paid to pillow fight.

   c. She lost weight and is athletic now.

5. What is the definition of pillow fighting? Complete the sentence below by filling in the missing words you hear.

   It's a weapon-based _____ sport, with the weapon being a _____.

6. What else do we know about pillow fighting? Circle the correct answers.

   a. Fights last five minutes.

   b. Fighters can use a pillow or hands to hit.

   c. Fighters win when an opponent falls off the bed.

   d. Fighters can hit the opponent's shoulders.

7. What does Amanda's family think about her choice of sport? Write each family member's reaction in the chart below.

Family Member	Reaction
a. Amanda's mother	
b. Amanda's grandmother	
c. Amanda's father	

8. How does Amanda respond to negative comments about her choice of sport?

_____

_____

_____

DISCUSSION

   1. What do you think about Amanda's choice to pillow fight?
   2. What other kinds of physical activities can someone who is not athletic participate in?
   3. What kind of personality does someone need for this activity?

WRITING FILES
Generating Ideas

What can help me to brainstorm ideas?
When you write about a topic, you may need to brainstorm or generate ideas first. To do this, you can use a graphic organizer. This helps you to write ideas that connect to your topic and to choose which specific topic to focus on.

Look at the example below. The central topic is in the middle circle, and the connecting ideas surround it.

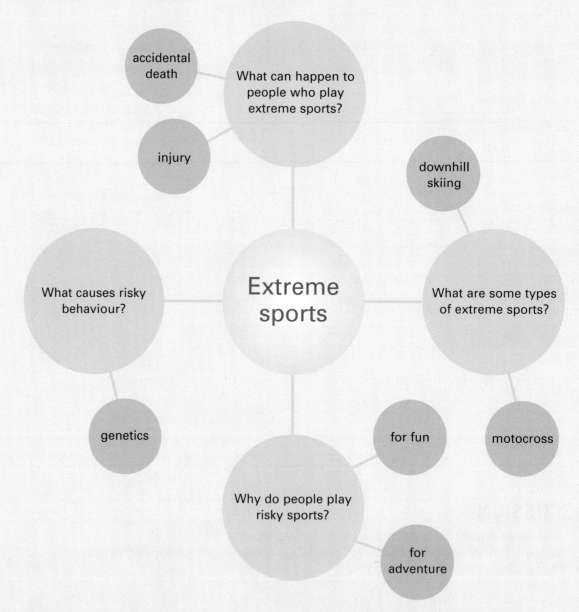

Brainstorm more ideas in small groups. How many more circles can you add?

Generate your own ideas for one of the topics below. Consult the checklist before you write.

physical activities and health	**competition**	**unusual sports**
sports addiction	**video gaming**	**exercise and socializing**

Make sure to follow these steps:

☐ Select a topic and write it in the middle of the graphic organizer.

☐ Add ideas that connect to the central topic. You may need to add more circles.

☐ Avoid writing ideas that do not connect to the central topic.

☐ Do not worry about spelling or grammar errors when you generate ideas.

☐ Select which circle you want to focus on. It will usually be the one that you can develop the most.

☐ Use this strategy whenever you have to brainstorm during writing and speaking activities.

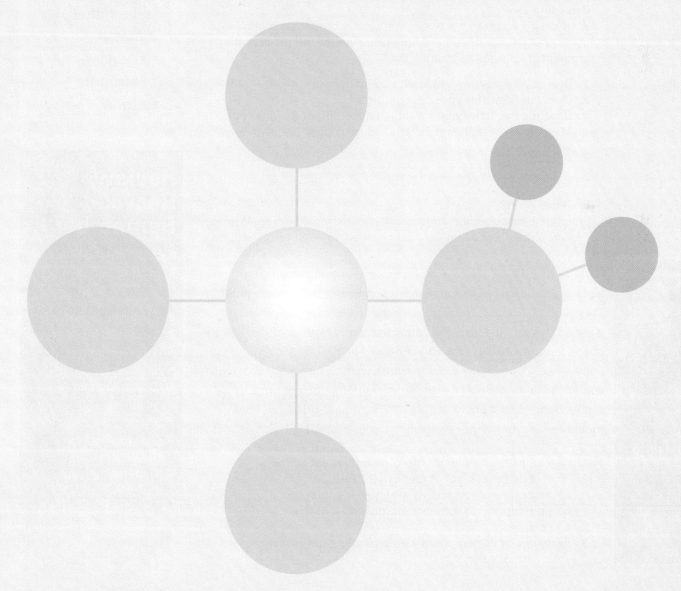

Project 1

Ad Writing

With a partner, create an advertisement for an upcoming sports event.

1. Choose a sports event to promote.
2. Include details (date, time, location, contact information, etc.) to describe the event. *Wheelchair Athletics **is having** a race. They **are raising** money for a charity.*
3. Write two or three sentences of a previous champion's personal testimony.
4. Make a logo and write a slogan.

 Project 2

Reporting Live

With a partner, present a two-minute radio broadcast of a new kind of sports competition or fitness activity taking place at the moment. You are broadcasting live!

1. Decide on a new kind of sports competition.
2. Generate ideas for your presentation.
3. Describe the activity and what is happening at the moment.
4. Make your presentation as interesting as possible. You may want to add sound effects.

📖 **Project 3**

Extreme What?

Read the blog about the unusual sport of extreme ironing. Write a paragraph to describe an unusual or little-known physical activity.

Here is a picture of a person doing extreme ironing in Canada. He is ice climbing and holding an ironing board at the same time! This extreme ironer is ironing his shirt at a high altitude, and wearing a helmet and ice picks attached to the bottom of his boots. Extreme ironing started in England in 1997 and is now popular worldwide. Why would anyone want to iron while playing sports? It allows people to exercise while doing their chores. It can be done almost anywhere—while horseback riding, climbing mountains, scuba diving, even while bungee jumping.

1. Research an unusual or little-known physical activity.
2. Write a paragraph about the activity. Include:
   a. the origins of the activity and how it is played
   b. a description of someone participating in the activity
   c. a picture
3. Exchange your paragraph with a partner, and respond to your partner's text.

Top Words

Put a check mark next to the words you know and learn the ones you do not remember.

- ☐ to apply
- ☐ to create*
- ☐ a demand
- ☐ fewer
- ☐ gaming
- ☐ to handle
- ☐ a match
- ☐ risk-taking
- ☐ to struggle
- ☐ to train

Review, Recycle, Remember

Incorporate the following items into your project files where appropriate.

- ■ Present progressive
- ■ Vocabulary and *In Words* relating to fitness
- ■ Skimming and scanning
- ■ Finding the main idea
- ■ Supporting your statement
- ■ Generating ideas

Information
EVOLUTION

How does technology shape a GENERATION?

What were some important
inventions of past generations?

How do older people adapt
to changing technology?

Does technology help solve
problems or create new ones?

In this unit, you will learn how
technology changes the way you live.

UNIT 3

ON THE SAME WAVELENGTH

For interactive online activities and other resources, go to **ODILON** www.cheneliere.ca/esl

 WARM-UP

Then And Now

What **technology** from your parents' or grandparents' generation brings back **memories** of the past? What technology replaces it **today**?

Read each activity below and technology associated with it in the past. Then, in the Now column, brainstorm the types of technology that you use now to do the same activity.

LANGUAGE LINK

Expressions to Indicate the Past

Use these expressions to talk about past actions and habits: *in those days, back then, before, a long time ago, used to.*

People **used to** listen to music on cassette tapes **back then**.

Telegrams were sent **a long time ago**.

Refer to Grammar Book, Unit 5.

Activity	Then	Now
1. She **called** me this morning.	rotary phone, landline telephone	
2. They **watched** a movie.	old-fashioned movie projector, black-and-white TV, VCR	
3. He **wrote** a letter.	handwritten letter, typewriter	
4. We **took** lots of pictures.	Polaroid camera, film cameras	
5. I **listened** to a few songs.	record player, cassette player	
6. I **copied** the song.	cassette recorder	
7. We **chatted** for hours.	telephone	
8. He **reported** the news.	newspaper, radio, television	

Talk about the above technology with a partner. Say what people used then and what they use now. Use the simple past and simple present when speaking.

Muriel's Message

This **award-winning** audio segment from CBC *Outfront* features the story of a young woman who describes the **memories** of her much-loved grandmother. An **old audio cassette**, labelled Muriel's Message, helps bring back these memories.

VOCABULARY

Match each word or expression with its correct definition before you listen.

1. to spoil someone		**a.** an audio cassette
2. a tape		**b.** to think about
3. a memory		**c.** as soon as possible
4. to call right back		**d.** to give someone a lot of attention and care
5. a basement		**e.** a part of a house that is underground
6. to wonder		**f.** a thought about a person or situation from the past
7. a neighbour		**g.** to write quickly in a messy manner
8. to scribble		**h.** someone who lives near or beside you

Make sure you understand the definitions of the words and expressions in bold before you listen.

played **in a loop** → continuously

Lewis Carroll → author of the popular children's classic *Alice in Wonderland*

Listen to the first part of the story and answer the questions below.

1. What is the main idea in this first part? Circle the correct answer.

a. Muriel loved her granddaughter very much.

b. A young woman finds an audio tape and remembers her grandmother.

c. Mira's grandmother, Muriel, was an incredible woman.

2. What did Mira find?

_____

3. Who is Muriel in relation to Mira?

_____

4. How did Muriel die? How old was she?

_____

5. What kind of grandmother was Muriel? Circle all the correct answers.

a. She was an artist.

b. She was a single mom at age 50.

c. She was active even at an old age.

d. She was unsociable.

6. Why does Mira think that her grandmother spoiled her?

_____

7. What do you think the message on the tape is? Write your prediction.

_____

How to...

Predict Events

Think about what you already know. This will help you to connect information and make predictions. Then describe what you think could have happened.

To support your predictions, use:

I think, maybe, probably, might

I think her tape **probably** contained her last will and testament.

Listen to the second part of the story and answer the questions below.

1. What was Muriel's message?

_____

_____

2. What was Muriel's old phone number? _____

3. Was the message on the tape what Mira expected? How did Mira feel after she first listened to the tape?

_____

_____

4. What did the message help Mira to remember after she listened to the recording a few times? Circle all the correct answers.

a. She remembered taking the bus to her grandmother's house.

b. She remembered climbing the huge crabapple tree.

c. She remembered how her grandmother smelled of soap and gum.

d. She remembered going for ice cream with her grandmother.

5. Why do you think the tape reminded Mira of her grandmother more than the photos on the refrigerator door?

_____

WRITING
Memories

Is there a **technology** from the **past** that helps you to **remember** a certain **family** member?

Write a paragraph about a memory from your childhood about a grandparent or other family member. Use the simple past in your writing.

 READING

Buyer Beware

Technology today allows us to **buy and sell** things easily on the Internet. You can find many **strange items** online. One man, Ian Usher, sold his **entire life** on eBay. Before you learn about his story, read about some unusual items sold on **eBay**.

Read the text below. Write the simple past form of the verbs in parentheses.

LANGUAGE LINK

Simple Past

Use the simple past for actions in the past that are completely finished.

Regular verbs end in *-d* or *-ed.*

*They **lived** in an old house.*

Pay attention to irregular verbs.

*We **had** many old records when we **were** teenagers.*

Refer to Grammar Book, Unit 5.

The Strangest eBay Auctions

1. **Girlfriends.** Some girls **(auction)** _auctioned_____ themselves as imaginary girlfriends.

   They **(send)** _____ the winner pictures of themselves so he could pretend to

   have a girlfriend.

2. **Wedding dress.** A man **(try)** _____ to sell his ex-wife's wedding dress. He even

   (model) _____ it. It **(sell)** _____ for about $7,000.

3. **Kidney.** One man **(try)** _____ to sell his kidney on eBay, but it is illegal to buy

   or sell human organs.

4. **Toenails.** A girl once **(sell)** _____ her cut toenails on eBay and **(get)**

   _____ $1 for the entire set.

5. **Britney's gum.** Someone **(pick)** _____ up Britney Spears' chewed gum at

   a London hotel and **(think)** _____ they could sell it on eBay. They **(be)**

   _____ right because they **(get)** _____ $263 for it!

6. **Ghost.** A man **(decide)** _____ to capture the ghost that **(haunt)**

   _____ him and sell it on eBay.

Michelle and Jesse Bendit are now friends.
30 Michelle is home.

No word from my daughter, though.

Out of the blue, I got an invitation to be a friend from one of my neighbours, Ted, who coincidentally had just joined to check out the
35 applications that independent software developers started adding to the site last month. He showed me how to add movie reviews and **snippets** of music to my profile.

I invited my friends—my actual friends—to
40 join Facebook. Some did. I sent a "**poke**" to one to say hello. I wrote on another's "wall." I tagged a photo to make it appear on my friend Tina's profile. In gratitude, she "poked" me.

Things were going really well, when sudden-
45 ly something disturbing happened. An instant-

message window appeared onscreen to deliver a verdict.

"way **creepy,**" it said. "why did you make one!"
50 Ah, there she was.

"What are you talking about?" I typed innocently.

"im only telling you for your own good," my daughter typed.
55 "Be my friend," I typed.

"You won't get away with this," she typed. "everyone in the whole world thinks its super creepy when adults have facebooks."

"Have facebooks? Is that what you think a
60 Profile page is called?" I typed.

She disconnected.

creepy → strange
out of the blue → all of a sudden

snippets → small amounts

poke → a way to get someone's attention online

Answer the questions below.

1. What is the main idea in Part 1? Circle the correct answer.

   a. Facebook only allows people to accept their friends into a social network.

   b. A mother tries using Facebook for the first time.

   c. A mother tries to convince her daughter to be her Facebook friend.

2. Which statement about the author is *false*? Circle the correct answer.

   a. She searched for new friends right after she joined Facebook.

   b. Her daughter's friends did not give her access to their profiles.

   c. She got an invitation from one of her neighbours.

3. Why was the author's daughter angry?

_____

4. Why did the author's daughter disconnect from Facebook during their online conversation?

_____

5. Write a question in the simple past to ask for the information in bold.

   a. I joined Facebook **last week**.

_____

   b. No, my daughter did not accept my invitation.

_____

6. Do you think the author's daughter accepts her mother as a friend? Write your prediction and support it with examples from the text.

_____

_____

_____

LANGUAGE LINK

Question Formation in the Simple Past

To form questions in the simple past, use the auxiliary *did* and the base form of the verb.

*Why **did** she **disconnect**?*
(Why did she ~~disconnected~~?)

Do not use an auxiliary with the verb *be*.

*Where **were** you yesterday?*
(Where ~~did you were~~ yesterday?)

Refer to Grammar Book, Unit 5.

Match each word or expression in bold with its correct definition before you watch.

1. wired	**a.** earlier
2. two weeks **ago**	**b.** to permit
3. thoughtful	**c.** not focused
4. incoming	**d.** kind, considerate
5. distracted	**e.** email or calls you receive
6. to allow	**f.** a meeting with someone you like romantically
7. a date	**g.** connected to a computer or other device

Make sure you understand the definitions of the words in bold before you listen.

to draw a blank → to not be able to think of the answer

a gadget → a small electronic device

at lightening speed → very quickly

Watch the video and answer the questions below.

1. What is the main idea of the video? Circle the correct answer.

   a. It costs a lot to use the latest email and cellphone technology.

   b. Cellphones and email are convenient, but they cause new problems for society.

   c. Technology is very bad for communication, and we need to control it.

2. Complete this sentence by circling the correct answer.

   The majority of people interviewed check their email: often   sometimes   rarely

3. What did Jesse Hirsh say about letter writing? Circle the correct answer.

    a. Writing a letter is more thoughtful, and more care is put into a letter than into an email.

    b. The language used in a letter contains more slang and is less concerned with correct English.

    c. Writing a letter is the same as writing an email.

4. What does George Stromboulopoulos use F7 for?

_____

_____

5. What does Beverly Beuermann-King, stress and wellness specialist, say are some of the effects of using email and cellphones?

_____

_____

_____

6. What do these people say about interrupting a conversation to check email or answer a cellphone? Write the correct number beside the name.

People Interviewed	Answers	Their Opinions
a. George Stromboulopoulos		**1.** This person would not interrupt a meeting with clients but would interrupt a meeting with other colleagues.
b. Debra Bain		**2.** This person would read an email during a conversation but would not send one.
c. Jesse Hirsh		**3.** This person would interrupt a conversation, but it also depends on who else is there.

7. What advice is given about using technology in the two situations below? Complete the chart.

Situation	Advice
a. On a date	
b. In a meeting or classroom	

8. What does Beverly Beuermann-King say about using technology such as a cellphone, pager, or email? Circle the correct answer.

    a. We need to use technology as a tool so that we do not become a slave to it.

    b. Set specific times to use this technology.

    c. Do not answer calls and emails or check your pager immediately.

    d. All of the above are correct.

SPEAKING

Is It **Worth** It?

Technology helps a lot of people, but it also causes **new problems**. Can you think of any?

Brainstorm with a partner two problems that technological devices solve, and two problems they create. Write your ideas in point form.

	Problems They Solve	Problems They Create
1. Cellphones	**a.** can be used in an emergency	**a.** interrupt conversations
	b.	**b.**
2. Computers	**a.**	**a.**
	b.	**b.**
3. Other technological device	**a.**	**a.**
	b.	**b.**

DISCUSSION

1. What are the pros and cons of technology? Refer to How to... as a guide for your discussion.

How to...

Express Pros and Cons

Use the expressions in bold to express the positive and negative sides of an issue.

On the one hand, cellphones help us to communicate easily. On the other hand, they cause a lot of interruptions.

Cars are very useful. For one thing, cars help us get somewhere fast. However, gas is very expensive.

Although debit cards are very easy to use, sometimes people lose them.

WRITING FILES
Paragraphs and Topic Sentences

What is a paragraph?
The purpose of a paragraph is to introduce one central idea. The topic sentence expresses this central idea and is usually the first sentence of the paragraph. A paragraph also consists of sentences that support or give information about the topic sentence.

How do I write a topic sentence?
1. Identify your topic and narrow it down.
2. Focus on one central idea. It should be a point of view or an opinion about the topic.

Topic Sentence

Topic	Central Idea
Online social networks	are not just for young people anymore.

3. Make sure your topic sentence is not too general. Otherwise, it will be difficult to focus on just one theme.
4. Make sure your topic sentence is not too specific. Otherwise, you will not have enough ideas to support it.

Read these sentences and indicate if the topic sentences are too specific, too general, or correct.

Topic Sentences	Too Specific	Too General	Correct
1. Everybody uses a cellphone nowadays.			
2. My grandfather is over 90 years old, and he has an iPod.			
3. Nobody uses a rotary phone anymore.			
4. Digital cameras can store a lot of pictures.			
5. Debits cards are convenient but come with their own set of problems.			

Identify and circle the topic sentence in the following paragraph.

A cellphone can help save a life. Your cellphone can also be used as a medical

ID bracelet. Software that allows you to store medical records on your phone now exists.

If you are lost, newer cellphones with GPS software can save your life by helping you

to determine where you are. Some companies and schools use cellphones to alert

people about emergencies, natural disasters, child abductions, or terrorist attacks.

Circle the best topic sentence below to introduce this paragraph. Read the paragraph first.

Facebook allows people to include their birth date, relationship status, and even details about their job! Younger people do not seem to worry much about privacy. The older crowds on Facebook do not share personal information as easily. However, there is no need to worry—Facebook only allows people who have been accepted as friends to see all the details of a profile.

a. Privacy is a real concern with Facebook.

b. Age plays a role in how much we reveal about ourselves on Facebook.

c. Only people who have been accepted as friends can see a Facebook profile.

Write a topic sentence for each of the topics below.

1. How technology improves our lives

_____

_____

2. Older people and technology

_____

_____

3. The negative aspects of technology

_____

_____

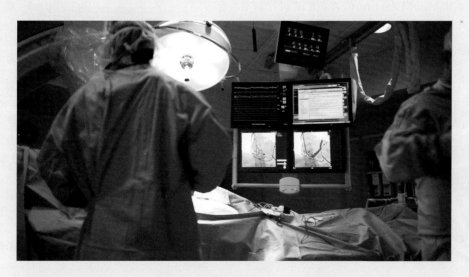

Project 1

Technology Week

Write about how technology affected your life this past week. How did technology help? What problems did technology cause for you or someone in your family?

1. Write a paragraph about your week.
2. Start with a good topic sentence.
3. Use the simple past. Include the negative forms.

 Project 2

Photographic Memory

Present a past event by showing your pictures to a small group.

1. Bring in some pictures from a past event, such as a wedding, graduation, family, trip, or party.
2. Talk about what happened.
3. Use the simple past. Include the negative forms.
4. Ask a few questions in the simple past about your presentation to see if your group remembered the details of your presentation.

 Project 3

Then and Now

Present the evolution of a certain type of technology, such as the evolution of technology related to music, movies, or computers.

1. Read about a type of technology of your choice.
2. Find out who invented it, when, and for what purpose.
3. Study how this technology has changed over time. Make a timeline with some important dates.
4. Use the simple past. Include the negative forms.
5. Ask a few questions in the simple past about your presentation to see if your group remembered the details of your presentation.

Top Words

Put a check mark next to the words you know and learn the ones you do not remember.

- ☐ to accomplish
- ☐ to achieve*
- ☐ ago
- ☐ to allow
- ☐ available*
- ☐ a date
- ☐ entire
- ☐ no longer
- ☐ a memory
- ☐ to wonder

Review, Recycle, Remember

Incorporate the following items into your project files where appropriate.

- ■ Simple past and expressions referring to the past
- ■ Vocabulary and *In Words* related to technology
- ■ Choosing the correct definition in a dictionary
- ■ Reading for details
- ■ Expressing pros and cons
- ■ Paragraphs and topic sentences

Into the
UNKNOWN

Looking at mysterious stories of the **PARANORMAL**

**What do Canadians believe
about the supernatural world?**

**Do you have an unexplainable
and mysterious story to tell?**

How do legends become popular?

**In this unit, you will express your
beliefs about the paranormal.**

UNIT 4

OUT OF THIS WORLD

respondent → person who takes a survey

ranked → in a certain order

former → first item in a list just mentioned

spokeswoman → woman who speaks for and represents others

flaky → unreliable or not serious

grounded → rational

gender bias → an attitude that prefers either the male or female gender

25 Most surprising to Smith was the fact that Atlantic Canada did not lead the country in either belief in the paranormal or belief that a supernatural presence was in the **respondent**'s home. In the latter category, the region **ranked** 30 fourth behind Alberta, Ontario, and Saskatchewan/Manitoba; in the **former** category, Atlantic Canada ranked fourth behind Saskatchewan/Manitoba, Alberta, and British Columbia.

"When I phoned to get Maritime stories (of 35 hauntings), it almost seemed if you didn't have a ghost, your house wasn't much of a home," says Smith. "I think it is the history of the sea and so many deaths... the *Titanic* sank just off the coast of Newfoundland."

40 The survey found that women are far more likely to believe in angels than men: 75 per cent versus 56 per cent. Age, however, had little influence over Canadians' faith in spiritual beings. Those aged 35 to 54 are only slightly more like-45 ly to believe in angels (68 per cent) than older (65 per cent) and younger (64 per cent) people.

A **gender bias** also was evident when it came to belief in spirits and ghosts: 53 per cent of women believe in the paranormal, compared to 50 42 per cent of men. Age made a big difference in this category, with younger (54 per cent) and

middle-aged Canadians (52 per cent) believing more than older people (39 per cent).

As a **spokeswoman** for Fort Edmonton Park, 55 an Alberta attraction famous for its paranormal activity, Jan Archbold has heard many ghost stories—particularly in relation to the Firkins House, a historical building.

"The previous owner had a number of 60 (supernatural) experiences in the house," says Archbold. "Sometimes it is easy for people to think, 'Well, they must be **flaky** if they're talking about those kinds of things,' but she was a very **grounded** individual."

65 Although Archbold has never witnessed anything paranormal personally, she does not reject the possibility of spirits.

"The city doesn't want us to emphasize the ghost part because we're here to provide the 70 historical perspective," she says. "But I myself am a spiritual kind of person and believe there is something far greater than what we know here."

Answer the questions below.

1. From where does the article get its information?

_____

2. Which statement is *false*? Circle the correct answer.
   a. More people believe in angels than ghosts and spirits.
   b. Ten per cent of people think their houses are haunted.
   c. Smith thinks the survey results are too high.

3. What kind of books did Barbara Smith write?

_____

FYI

There are lots of haunted places in Quebec and across Canada. Did you know that a college in the Gaspé is haunted? Read all about an old hotel, Le Château Frontenac, another ghostly building. Refer to Project Files, page 76.

4. Scan the text and fill in the chart with the percentages for each category.

	Believe in Angels	Believe in Ghosts and Spirits
a. Men	56%	
b. Women		
c. Younger people		
d. Middle-aged people		
e. Older people		

5. Complete the sentences by using the information from the chart in Question 4.

   a. More than half of men believe in _____ .

   b. About one-third of younger people don't believe in _____ .

   c. About one in two middle-aged people believe in _____ .

   d. Older people are more likely to believe in _____ than

      in _____ .

6. Which of these provinces or regions ranked last in believing in the paranormal?

   a. Alberta

   b. Atlantic Canada

   c. Ontario

   d. Saskatchewan/Manitoba

7. Which quote tells us that Jan Archbold thinks paranormal activity is possible?

_____

_____

DISCUSSION

   1. What is your reaction to the results of the survey? Refer to the chart in Question 4.
   2. Which results surprised you the most?

IN WORDS

Word Families
A word can change its form when it is a verb, noun, or adjective. Prefixes, such as *-un*, can make words negative.

Complete the missing forms of the words for each of the word families below.

	Verb	Noun	Adjective	Negative Adjective
1.		a belief		unbelievable
2.	to haunt	a haunting		X
3.		a scare	scary/scared	X
4.	to fear		fearful	X
5.	to predict		predictable	
6.		an education		uneducated

Circle the correct form of the word in the sentences below.

Rachel did not (believe / belief)[1] in ghosts or (haunting / haunted)[2] houses. As a child, she was never (scare / scared)[3] of the dark. She was not (fear / fearful)[4] of the unknown. She also did not think that psychics could make (predict / predictions)[5] about the future. She considered herself an (educated / education)[6] person. Some studies show that many people have a strong (believe / belief)[7] in the paranormal, especially those with a higher (educated / education)[8].

▣ WATCHING

The Legend of the Flying Canoe

This NFB animated film features a well-known **Quebec legend** from 1891, written by Honoré Beaugrand. What happens to a group of loggers who **cannot return home** because of the heavy snowfall just before **New Year's Eve**?

VOCABULARY

Circle the correct definition for each word and expression below before you watch.

1. to be snowed in	**a.** to be inside an igloo	**b.** to be unable to travel because of the snow
2. a pact	**a.** a box	**b.** a deal
3. a sunrise	**a.** morning sun	**b.** sunshine
4. dawn	**a.** early morning	**b.** just before evening
5. to swear	**a.** to make a promise	**b.** to lie

Make sure you understand the definitions of the words in bold before you watch.

a logger → a person whose job is to cut down trees
a paddle → a wooden piece that is used to move a canoe through water
to be scared out of our wits → to be very afraid

Watch the short film and answer the questions below.

1. What did Baptiste propose when the loggers were snowed in?

_____

_____

2. Why did they risk taking the flying canoe?

_____

_____

3. What two conditions did they need to respect in order to use the flying canoe and return home safely?

_____

_____

4. Put a check mark in the T or F column to indicate if the statement is _true_ or _false_.

	T	F
a. Lavaltrie was six hundred miles away from the loggers' camp.		
b. The Flying Canoe flew over a hundred miles an hour.		
c. To use the canoe, the men just had to watch what they were saying.		
d. The canoe almost crashed and Baptiste fell out.		

5. How did the loggers know they were travelling in bad company? Circle the correct answer.
  a. Baptiste was drinking too much at the party.
  b. It was a bad idea to make a pact with the Devil.
  c. They regretted going to the New Year's Eve party.

6. What story did the loggers tell to explain Baptiste's disappearance? Circle the correct answer.
  a. Baptiste was about to swear so they pushed him out of the canoe.
  b. They said he took a job in a neighbouring town.
  c. No one knew what happened to him and they never saw him again.

7. What is the moral of the story?

_____

Many cultures relied on storytelling or oral traditions to pass on their traditions and cultural knowledge. Stories were told to teach children, instruct moral values, or simply to entertain. There are storytelling competitions even today—such as the Quebec Intercultural Storytelling Festival.

📖 READING

An Unexplainable Story

Did you experience an **unusual** or unexplainable event in the past that did not have a logical explanation? If so, **you are not alone**!

VOCABULARY

Match each word with its correct definition before you read. The line number is in parentheses.

1. to compromise (31)	a. strange, scary
2. to beg (49)	b. to jump
3. to manage (52)	c. to ask or insist on something
4. to leap (53)	d. personal possessions
5. creepy (56)	e. to be able to deal with something
6. belongings (62)	f. to make a deal, negotiate

Practise the vocabulary words by writing two sentences. You may include more than one word per sentence.

1. _____

_____

2. _____

_____

Read the story.

The Case of the Leaping Book

rightful → correct one

thud → sound something makes on impact

brewed → boiled drink like tea or coffee

tome → book

We all experience strange, unusual phenomena at least once in our lives. This true, perhaps unbelievable account has no explana-
5 tion to date. Some choose to believe it, others simply say it is a strange coincidence.

I remember well that summer when I moved to my second apartment in Rosemont. I recently turned 20 after graduating from college that
10 same spring. My roommate Beverly was a single mother who needed the extra cash from a roommate because she was trying to save money.

It was a hot sticky August evening. I was just finishing up unpacking the few boxes of per-
15 sonal items and my numerous books. I love to read books of the horror genre. I remember after reading *The Amityville Horror*, a novel based on a supposedly true story, I awoke at 3:15 a.m. without any explanation for about
20 three weeks in a row. Incidentally, the murders were committed at that time in the story.

While I was unpacking, Beverly noticed one of my books, *The Eyes of Laura Mars*. She was very unhappy about having these kinds of books in
25 her house, because she was a regular churchgoer, and this was contrary to her religious beliefs. Furthermore, she believed the books carried the spirits of those written about them. As a rational person, I tried to dismiss her fears, but Beverly
30 was not easily convinced. "Alright," I said, trying to compromise, "let me at least return it to its **rightful** owner." This particular book belonged to my friend Kathy from college, whom I had not seen in a long time. I decided to give it back as
35 soon as I saw her again.

It was nine in the evening and the violet sky was slowly getting dark, as it usually does during the Montreal summer. I had finally put most of my things away and had tightly squeezed my
40 books into a bookshelf. Sometime in the night, while I was sleeping, I heard a light **thud**. Perhaps the cat had jumped off the desk. I quickly returned to sleep.

The kitchen sounds of cups clanging and the
45 aroma of a freshly **brewed** coffee later woke me from a deep sleep. Beverly poked her head into the room and offered a delicious breakfast. "Please, pick that book off the floor," she begged. She told me she did not like the eyes on
50 the cover staring back at her. Surely enough, in some unexplainable way, that same book, *The Eyes of Laura Mars*, had managed somehow to leap off the shelf and onto the floor. I clearly remembered it squeezed between my other
55 books after I unpacked. This strange incident was quite creepy so I immediately tossed the spooky **tome** into the trash bin. Was this the end of the story? Well, no.

A few months later, my sister reminded me
60 that my parents needed to renovate the spare

bedroom and they asked me to come clear away the rest of my belongings. I always enjoyed visiting my childhood home in the **suburbs**. My sister was helping me gather the few books into 65 a box when something caught my eye. There, on a shelf, in my parents' house, 30 kilometres from my Rosemont apartment, was *The Eyes of Laura Mars*, the same book I had thrown out five months earlier. Kathy's name was still written 70 inside. My skin was covered with **goosebumps**. Without any hesitation, I threw that book out a second time. It has not reappeared since.

suburbs → neighbourhoods near a city

goosebumps → raised bumps on the skin when cold or afraid

Answer the questions below.

1. How does the author let us know that this could be a ghost story?

_____

_____

2. What strange event happened to the author before she moved in with Beverly?

_____

_____

3. What is the correct order of these events in the story? Put them into chronological order (1-4).

a. _____ The author threw away the book a second time.

b. _____ The book leapt out of the bookcase at night.

c. _____ The author threw away the book.

d. _____ The book showed up in the author's parents' house.

4. How did the author know for sure that it was the same book she threw out?

_____

_____

5. Scan the text for six different words with the prefix *un-* and write them below:

_____

6. Look at the title. What is the function of the prefix *un-* ?

_____

7. The author uses adjectives that involve the senses; for example: *It was a hot sticky August evening*. Find more examples in the text.

a. sight	violet sky
b. hearing	
c. taste	
d. touch	
e. smell	

8. Find five verbs in the past progressive and underline them.

LANGUAGE LINK

Using the Possessive 's

Add the *'s* to a word to show possession. Remember to put the apostrophe after the *-s* for words that end in *-s*.

My friend's book was in my parents' house.

Refer to Grammar Book, Unit 3.

LANGUAGE LINK

Past Progressive

Form the past progressive by using the auxiliary *was* or *were*, and the base form of the verb with an *-ing* ending.

We were watching the show.

The negative is formed by adding *not* after the auxiliary.

He was not listening to my story.

To make a question, place the auxiliary before the subject.

Are you waiting for us?

Refer to Grammar Book, Unit 6.

 WRITING

What Really Happened?

Write a short paragraph to explain why you do or do not believe this story. If you are skeptical, what do you think are some possible explanations for this strange event?

_____

_____

_____

_____

_____

SPEAKING

Your Story

Do you have an **unusual story** to tell? Tell a story about something unexplainable **that happened to you** or to someone you know, or share a **strange story** you read about.

Tell your story in small groups. Remember to use the simple past and past progressive.

PRONUNCIATION

Silent Letters
Some words contain letters that we do not pronounce. Here are a few of the main ones. Listen to the list of words with silent letters below.

Silent Letters	Words with Silent Letters
B	thum**b**, lam**b**, clim**b**, plum**b**er
G	si**g**n, desi**g**n
H	**g**host, **h**our, **h**onest
L	wa**l**k, ta**l**k, cou**l**d, wou**l**d
K	**k**now, **k**nee, **k**night, **k**nife, **k**nit
S	i**s**land
T	cas**t**le, whis**t**le, lis**t**en, balle**t**, chale**t**, debu**t**
W	**w**rite, **w**ho, **w**rist, **w**rong

Listen to these sentences that contain words with silent letters. Cross off the silent letters.

1. The ghost was hiding high up above the house.

2. The amber spider was climbing on the plumber's thumb.

3. I listened as the wind was whistling outside the castle.

4. Who was writing with a broken wrist?

5. He wasn't doing ballet at the chalet.

6. She was walking calmly while I was talking about what we would do.

7. The knight knew the enemy was holding a knife.

8. I saw the desert island in the distance.

Read the sentences above aloud with a partner. Make sure you do not pronounce the silent letters.

 READING

A Ghost Story

What if your **earliest memories** included a **ghost**? A once-famous actress from the silent movie era revisits her old dressing room.

VOCABULARY

Circle the correct definition for each word and expression below before you read. The line number is in parentheses.

1. to convert (7)	**a.** to transform	**b.** to redecorate
2. an income (11)	**a.** a bill	**b.** salary
3. privacy (12)	**a.** a secret	**b.** a desire to be alone
4. rent (21)	**a.** payment for an apartment, etc.	**b.** bank payment
5. lace (43)	**a.** a shiny material	**b.** a delicate material
6. a closet (45)	**a.** a small room to put clothes	**b.** a door
7. to reveal (79)	**a.** to show	**b.** to hide
8. envious (88)	**a.** jealous	**b.** evil

Don't:
Immediately use a dictionary to understand words you do not know in a text.

Do:
Guess what the word means by looking at it in context.

Look at the new word to see if it looks like another word you know (**know**ledge).

Identify the part of speech (noun, verb, etc.) to help understand its function.

Look for words that you know before and after the new word to help you understand it.

staircase → set of stairs

blinked → opened and closed both eyes

drifted to sleep → fell asleep

to die for → to strongly desire something

boarding house → house with many rooms to rent

embroidery → decorative designs sewn on material

Guess the meaning of these words from their context. The line numbers of the text are in parentheses to help you. Check your answers in the dictionary.

1. to work out (10)

2. to overhear (17)

3. a recluse (19)

4. to elude (48)

5. a sighting (71)

6. threatened (73)

Read the story.

The Ghost of Pearl White

Retold by S. E. Schlosser
AmericanFolklore.net

When I was a kid, my grandparents bought a huge old **boarding house** in Jersey City. It had once housed the actresses working for
5 a big silent film studio across the street, but the film studio was long gone, and the boarding house was unused. My grandparents converted it into a three-family home. They moved into the bottom floor, offered my parents the sec-
10 ond floor, and rented out the third. It worked out pretty good for everyone. Extra income for my grandparents, privacy for our family with quick access to Grandma when it was wanted or needed, and the couple on the third floor
15 were quiet. Very quiet.

Not sure where I got the notion from—maybe I overheard my parents talking—but I soon got it into my young head that the wife of the man renting the apartment upstairs was a recluse. My

20 parents never saw her, and when it was time to pay the rent, it was the man who walked downstairs to the ground floor to speak to my grandparents. We all thought it a bit strange that the woman was so unsocial, but other school con-
25 cerns quickly drove the woman out of my mind. At least for awhile.

Now bedtime for me, at the new house, was 8:00 p.m. sharp. My bedroom was opposite the **staircase**, and I could see it clearly when lying
30 tucked up in my bed for the night. So when the strange lady in the gorgeous, fancy yellow dress came walking past my room, and headed up toward the third floor staircase one night, I **blinked** for a moment in surprise. Then I real-
35 ized it must be the reclusive wife of our neighbour, and I relaxed. She sure was a pretty lady, I thought as I **drifted to sleep**. And that dress was **to die for**!

After that, I saw the lady most nights, walk-
40 ing past my door to the staircase. I loved her clothes. Often she wore the yellow dress. But sometimes it was blue or pink or white, with lovely lace or **embroidery**. One night, she came right into my room and went into the
45 closet. That surprised me a little. Then I realized there must be a secret staircase in my closet, leading to the third floor. In the morning I tried to find it, but it eluded me. I saw her walk into the closet a couple of times over the years, but
50 usually she just walked up the main staircase.

Eventually, my grandparents sold the house to my aunt, and all of us went to live in a nice home in the suburbs. About a month after the move, my aunt came to my parents' house in a rage. I sat in
55 the kitchen, eating cookies and listening quietly, hoping no one would notice me and send me away while they talked "grown-up" stuff.

"I can't believe you sold me a haunted house!" my aunt said to Grandpa.

60 "What do you mean, haunted?" Grandpa asked. And my aunt explained. In detail. About the ghostly woman who walked up the second floor staircases each night at eight, and who sometimes went into the closet of my old room.

65 I stared at her in wonder. The woman had been a ghost? Really? I could barely believe it. Still, my aunt had seen her, long after the couple on the third floor had moved away from the building. Feeling it was time to speak up, I told 70 my parents and grandparents about my own ghostly sightings. They had to believe it, since both my aunt and I had seen the ghost. I told my parents that I never felt threatened or frightened in any way when I saw the ghost. Indeed, my 75 memories of the ghost are all pleasant ones.

A look through old photographs of female stars of the old silent films identified the ghost as that of Pearl White, and further research revealed that my old closet had been the 80 **dressing room** for some of the actresses. So that explained why the ghost had sometimes walked into my closet, although I was a bit disappointed that there was no secret staircase.

To this day, I still have no idea why the ghost 85 of Pearl White still walks the halls of her old boarding house. Perhaps it is to remind herself of a happy period in her life. All I know for sure is that she has the best clothes! I'm still envious of her beautiful dresses.

dressing room → room where actors get dressed

Answer the questions below.

1. What is the main idea of the story? Circle the correct answer.
   a. An actress used to make silent movies and her dressing room was haunted.
   b. The author remembers living in an old converted boarding house.
   c. The author remembers a visitor who used to rent the third floor.
   d. An actress haunted an old house where the author used to live.

2. Who lived in the old house? Circle the correct answer.
   a. The author and her grandparents lived in the house on the second floor.
   b. The author lived above her grandparents and below the boarders.
   c. The author and her parents and the boarders all lived in the house.

3. What do we know about the mysterious woman? Circle the correct answer.
   a. She visited every night and often went into the author's dressing room.
   b. The mysterious woman was the boarder's wife and she was an actress.
   c. Her dresses were very beautiful and the author envied them.
   d. Her name was Pearl White and she still walks the halls of the old boarding house today.

4. Why was the aunt upset after she purchased the house?

   _____

5. When did the author realize the visitor was not the boarder's wife?

   _____

6. Why was the author not frightened of the nightly visitor?

   _____

DISCUSSION

1. Why do you think ghost stories are still popular in this age of science and technology?
2. What makes a good ghost story?

LISTENING

Paranormal Investigations

In this **interview**, Judith Lessitor, a member of the **Montreal Paranormal Group**, talks about her **real-life experiences** investigating haunted houses and other paranormal phenomena.

VOCABULARY

Circle the correct definition for the words below before you listen.

1. to solve	a. to figure out	b. to become liquid
2. to sense	a. to learn	b. to feel
3. to allow	a. to let	b. to give
4. to record	a. to write a song	b. to put information on film or tape
5. to vanish	a. to clean and polish	b. to disappear
6. a trail	a. lines or marks left by someone	b. a plate
7. to reassure	a. to repeat	b. to calm someone down
8. non-threatening	a. not dangerous	b. not confident
9. to warn	a. to make something hot	b. to tell someone about danger
10. to conduct	a. to carry out	b. to build

Make sure you understand the definitions of the words in bold before you listen.

floppy → soft, not solid

a nun → a woman in a religious order

pantaloons → large pants tied above the feet

well-manicured → clean and neatly cut

Listen to the interview and answer the questions below.

1. What is the main idea of the interview? Circle the correct answer.
   a. A paranormal investigator talks about her experiences with haunted houses.
   b. There are many haunted houses in Montreal.
   c. The Montreal Paranormal Group is for paranormal investigators.
   d. People interested in the paranormal should join this Meetup Group.

2. Which statement about the Montreal Paranormal Group is *false*? Circle the correct answer.
   a. Patrick Zakhm started the group.
   b. There are about 180 members in the group.
   c. The group sometimes solves a case, but not always.
   d. The Montreal Paranormal Group visits houses at night when no one is home.

3. Put a check mark in the T or F column to indicate if the statement is *true* or *false*.

	T	F
a. She used to hear stories about ghosts haunting old castles.		
b. She found out about the group when she was living in England.		
c. She was playing piano when she heard about the group.		
d. She was teaching and editing at the time.		

4. Describe the ghost the paranormal investigators saw at The Saint Gabriel in the Old Port. What verb tense is used to describe the ghost's clothing?

a. _____

_____

_____

b. _____

5. Which two statements about the investigations are *true*? Circle the correct answers.
   a. The group uses infrared cameras to film in the dark.
   b. The group uses special machines to record a ghost's presence.
   c. The ghosts are usually someone's imagination or even gases.
   d. The group uses old equipment that they trust.

6. Put the following events in the order that they took place.

   a. _____ A young boy living in the new house felt something on his pillow.

   b. _____ The owners called the Montreal Paranormal Group to investigate.

   c. _____ A boy living in the old house died in a fire.

   d. _____ The investigators believed that the boy's ghost was looking for a new family.

7. What other paranormal activity did the group see during an investigation?

_____

_____

8. What does Judith say about skeptics? Circle all the correct answers.
   a. The Montreal Paranormal Group may have skeptics who join.
   b. The Montreal Paranormal Group refuses skeptics who want to join.
   c. Skeptics always experience unusual events.
   d. Many skeptics are looking for answers to unexplained events in their lives.

DISCUSSION

   1. Did your beliefs about the paranormal change after listening to Judith? Explain.
   2. What are some examples of current movies, books, or television shows on the subject of paranormal? Are they popular? Why or why not?

Project 1

What's Your Position?
In small groups, choose one of the paranormal concepts from the Warm-Up, page 60. Decide which students in your group will be *for* or *against* the concept.

1. Do some research to find one article about your subject and to support your position.
2. Be prepared to speak about your position and to support it.
3. Present the information to other groups.

 Project 2

Mysterious Story
Write a short mysterious story, but do not finish the story.
A classmate will write the ending.

1. Start a short mysterious story but leave out the ending.
2. Your teacher will assign you another student's story to complete.
3. Write an ending for the story.
4. You could take turns reading your stories to the class.

 Project 3

Haunted Canada
Why do ghosts haunt a particular place? Was there a tragedy, such as a lost love, or some unfinished business that keeps them there?

1. Research a famous haunted place in Canada.
2. Write a paragraph to explain the story about the ghost.

One famous haunted site is the old hotel, Le Château Frontenac, in Quebec City. It was built in 1893 as the home for the governor of New France, Louis de Buade, Comte de Frontenac. Many people saw his ghost in the hotel. They report that he was wearing the clothes of that period. Sometimes he was just walking around, other times he was sitting on the windowsill. A few guests said he was staring at them while they were sleeping. Apparently, he is still looking for his fiancée. She was in France at the time of his death. Many people also saw a ghostly woman with long hair wearing a nightgown. Was this the fiancée of Louis de Buade, Comte de Frontenac?

Top Words

Put a check mark next to the words you know and learn the ones you do not remember.

- ☐ an author*
- ☐ a belief
- ☐ to convince*
- ☐ creepy
- ☐ to emphasize*
- ☐ faith
- ☐ to overhear
- ☐ to provide
- ☐ to reveal*
- ☐ to witness

Review, Recycle, Remember

Incorporate the following items into your project files where appropriate.

- ■ Simple past and past progressive
- ■ Vocabulary and *In Words* from the unit
- ■ Talking about beliefs
- ■ Getting meaning from context
- ■ Transition words

Communicate What You
MEAN

UNIT 5

How do you know if someone is lying to you?

What do people lie about on dating websites?

How easy is it for students to cheat?

In this unit, see if you agree with the experts about lying and cheating.

SPEAK YOUR MIND

For interactive online activities and other resources, go to ODILON
www.cheneliere.ca/esl

FYI

Reader's Digest conducted an honesty test. They dropped cellphones in cities all over the world to see who would keep them and who would return them to their owners. People in Toronto returned 28 out of the 30 dropped cellphones, coming in second place to the people of Ljubljana, in Slovenia.

LANGUAGE LINK

Worse, the Worst,* and *as Bad as

When you compare two things, use ***worse***.

*Stealing is **worse** than lying.*

When you compare more than two things, use ***the worst***.

***The worst** offence on the list is going over the speed limit.*

When two things are equally bad, use ***as bad as***.

*I think getting help on an essay is **as bad as** cheating.*

Refer to Grammar Book, Unit 7.

 WARM-UP

You Be the Judge

When is it **acceptable** to lie? Is honesty always **appropriate**?

Discuss the following situations with a partner and decide if they are acceptable, not acceptable or sometimes acceptable. Create two other situations. Put a check mark in the appropriate box.

Is It Acceptable to:	Yes	No	Sometimes
1. Help someone with an assignment?			
2. Take a pen from work?			
3. Park in a designated handicap parking space?			
4. Go over the speed limit?			
5. Sneak into a movie or concert without paying?			
6. Damage a car and not leave any contact information?			
7. Keep something you find?			
8. Tell a lie?			
9. Other:			
10. Other:			

DISCUSSION

1. Which situations are sometimes acceptable? Explain.
2. Which situation is the worst offence in your opinion? Explain.

How Can You Detect a Lie?

Many experts agree that you can tell if someone is **lying to you**. You just have to know what **signs to look for**.

Complete the chart below before you read the text. Fill in the missing vocabulary words from the text or the missing definitions. Use the line numbers in parentheses and a dictionary to help you.

	Vocabulary Word	Definition
1.	to lie (2)	
2.	to make up (16)	
3.		to not have (18)
4.	a clue (22)	
5.	to figure out (26)	
6.		to increase (30)
7.	behaviour (35)	
8.		truthful (37)
9.		a lie or an untruth (42)
10.		evidence (46)

Read the text once. Then read it again and highlight the essential information in each section. Next, match the subtitles from the list below to each section of the text.

Ask Again	**A Change in Voice**	~~**Eye Contact**~~	**Eye Movement**
Go with Your Feelings	**A Pause Before Speaking**	**Repeated Lies**	**A Short Story**
Stressed Out	**Trying to Convince**		

Top Ten Tips to Recognize a Liar

1. Eye Contact

People who lie do not feel comfortable with eye contact. Someone who cannot look you in the eye may be lying.

5 **2.** _____

Watch the eyes when you ask someone to tell you a memory or true event. Do the eyes go up to the left or to the right? The left side of the

How to...

Highlight Essential Information

When you read, it is important to highlight the main points and any important information. This helps you to summarize what you read.

1. Make sure to read the text at least once before you highlight.

2. Think about what was important in the text.

3. Read the text a second time, and then highlight important information. You do not need to highlight every word in a sentence.

4. When you finish, read the highlighted parts to see if they include the information you are looking for.

Using *Than* in Comparisons

Use *than* to compare two things.

Notice the wording of the comparisons in numbers 6 and 8 of the Top Ten list.

*It is much **harder** to remember a lie **than** the truth.*

*People who are honest feel **more relaxed than** those who are lying.*

Make sure to spell *than* correctly. (~~then~~)

Refer to Grammar Book, Unit 7.

pull the wool over your eyes → lie to you

brain controls memory. The right side controls
10 imagination. An honest person's eyes should go up to the right because the right side of the body is controlled by the left side of the brain.

3. _____
If the person pauses or hesitates after you ask
15 a question, it might be that the liar is looking for time to make up or invent a story.

4. _____
A liar's story usually lacks detail. A liar may also avoid using the pronoun "I." If you notice
20 this, be careful!

5. _____
Another clue to finding out a potential lie is to ask yourself if this person lied in the past.

6. _____
25 Ask to hear the story one more time at a later date. It is easy to figure out a lie when the stories do not match. It is much harder to remember a lie than the truth.

7. _____
30 The voice rises when someone is telling a lie. Listen for a voice that sounds higher than usual if you think someone is lying to you.

8. _____
Lying makes most people uncomfortable.
35 Watch out for unusual behaviour, like finger tapping or moving around in one's seat. People who are honest feel more relaxed than those who are lying.

9. _____
40 Many liars try to persuade you that they are being honest. Careful, they may be just telling you a big fib!

10. _____
Your instincts may be right. If it sounds like a
45 lie, it probably is! No one single sign alone is proof that someone is lying. But if you notice all of these signs, someone may be trying to pull the wool over your eyes.

SPEAKING

Who Is Telling the Truth?

Can you tell if someone is being truthful or telling a lie? This **lie-detector** game will give you a **chance to find out**!

Form groups of three. Tell one *true* story about an unusual or interesting event that happened to you in the past, and one *untrue* story that did not happen. Do not let the other members of your group know which story is true and which one is not true.

Observe the members of your group while you listen to their stories and write their behaviour in the chart below. Pay attention to their eyes, face, body, and hands.

Simple Past and Past Progressive

Use the **simple past** for actions in the past that are completely finished.

*I **tried** to climb Mount Kilimanjaro.*

Use the **past progressive** for actions in progress at a specific time in the past.

*While I **was climbing** the mountain, I got sick and did not complete the hike.*

Refer to Grammar Book, Units 5 and 6.

	Behaviour: Story 1	Behaviour: Story 2
Student 1		
Student 2		

DISCUSSION

1. Were you able to notice when a member of your group was lying?
2. How different was their behaviour when students lied or told the truth?
3. Is there a pattern you can observe when someone lies? Explain.

IN WORDS

Body Language

Your body language often changes when you tell a lie. In this activity, review the names of body parts and the verbs associated with them.

Write the name of the body part associated with each action described below. Then label each body part on the diagram.

How to...

Talk About Perceptions

Use the verbs *seem* or *appear* to talk about your perceptions.

It **seemed** to me that he was not telling the truth.

He **seemed** to pause before speaking.

She **appeared** to be looking to the left.

Verb	Body Part
1. to hug	arms
2. to hitchhike	
3. to look	
4. to walk	
5. to talk	
6. to listen	
7. to sneeze	
8. to wave goodbye	
9. to type an email	
10. to whistle	
11. to wear a tie or necklace	
12. to shrug when you are unsure	

arms

 WATCHING

Deception Detectives

In this video segment from CTV: *Canada AM*, you will **learn tips** from the experts on **how to detect dishonesty**.

VOCABULARY

Match each word or expression with its correct definition before you watch.

1. sneaky	**a.** past or earlier
2. to spot	**b.** to pause
3. previous	**c.** not at all
4. to get along with	**d.** a sign
5. anything but	**e.** not honest, indirect
6. an indicator	**f.** to have a good relationship
7. to mask	**g.** to detect
8. to stall	**h.** to hide

Make sure you understand the definitions of these terms.

HR → Human Resources

to retreat → to physically move away from

Watch the video and answer the questions below.

1. Put a check mark in the T or F column to indicate if the statement is *true* or *false*.

	T	F
a. Alan is a behavioural analyst.		
b. Kaaryn is a statement analyst.		
c. A statement analyst looks at body language.		
d. A behavioural analyst examines people's words.		

2. What comments do Kaaryn and Alan make about their role-play? Write your answers in the chart below.

	Answer to the First Question	Answer to the Second Question
	"It was great, it was just great—no problems there. We all got along great with the boss."	*"Why did I leave my previous employer? Well, I guess I just needed more of a challenge."*
Statement Analyst	**a.** He did not use the _____ pronoun. **b.** He did not use the pronoun _____ when speaking about the boss. **c.** He did not _____ the question.	**a.** He answered the question with a _____. **b.** He stalled to think of a _____.
Behavioural Analyst	**d.** His face: _____ **e.** His body: _____ **f.** His hands: _____ _____	**c.** His eyes: _____ _____

DISCUSSION

How does the behaviour of the students in your group during the "Who Is Telling the Truth?" activity compare with what the experts say in the video? Be specific. (Refer to the chart on page 80 to help you).

 READING

Dating Dishonesty

Are "**white lies**" acceptable in an online profile? What do you think people lie about the most on a **dating website**?

VOCABULARY

Circle the correct definition for each of the words in bold before you read.

1. They **improved** how they looked.   a. made better   b. liked

2. There were **gender** differences.   a. general   b. male or female

3. The **trait** most people lied about was weight.   a. characteristic   b. treat

4. People lied **least** about their age.   a. not often   b. very often

5. Some lies were **uncovered**.   a. acceptable   b. discovered

Avoid Overgeneralizations

When you speak or write, accuracy and precision are important. Avoid overgeneralizations like *everyone*, *always*, or *never*, unless it is absolutely true.

Many people lie on dating websites. (~~Everyone~~ lies...)

Women **sometimes** lie in their online profiles. (Women ~~always~~ lie...)

Men **don't usually** lie about their age. (Men ~~never~~ lie...)

Read the text.

Tall, Dark, and Dishonest

New Scientist

Dating websites seem like the perfect place to lie. Now a study that compared online profiles with real life has found that most daters fib, but only in 5 moderation.

"People were lying strategically. They told small lies that improved how they looked, but not so large that they would **get busted** if the daters met," says Jeff Hancock of Cornell 10 University in Ithaca, New York. His team weighed and measured 40 male and 40 female daters in New York City, noted the age on their driver's licence, and compared the results with their online profiles.

15 Nearly nine out of ten participants lied at least once, with weight the most lied-about trait and age the least. There were also gender differences: every woman who lied about her weight said she was lighter than she was, while 20 most men who lied about height made themselves taller. The heavier the women were, and the shorter the men, the more likely they were to tell fibs.

But while lies were frequent, the vast major-25 ity were unlikely to be uncovered in face-to-face meetings. The average difference between a profile and reality was a mere three kilograms in weight, one centimetre in height, and just five months in age.

30 It seems that online dating websites get their **bad rap** from a few really big lies, which are most likely to get talked about. The worst **whoppers** in Hancock's survey were eight centimetres in height, sixteen kilograms in weight, 35 and eleven years in age. "The big ones are much more memorable," he says.

get busted → get caught

bad rap → bad reputation

whopper → really big lie

FYI

Is it okay to tell a lie if nobody gets hurt? Some specialists say that "white lies" are fine when you want to protect someone you love. But they can hurt your relationship if you are trying to protect yourself.

Answer the questions below.

1. What is the main idea of the text? Circle the correct answer.

   a. Nearly nine out of ten participants lie on dating websites.

   b. People lie on dating websites, but they usually only tell small lies.

   c. It is important to be honest.

2. Why do people not tell big lies on dating websites?

_____

_____

3. Which statement is false? Circle the correct answer.

    a. All people surveyed lied at least once on dating sites.

    b. The trait most people lie about is weight.

    c. The trait the fewest people lie about is age.

    d. Both men and women lie on dating websites.

4. What do men and women lie about the most?

a. Men	
b. Women	

5. Scan the article and complete the chart.

	Average Lie	Worst Lie
a. Height		
b. Weight		16 kg
c. Age	5 months	

6. Scan the text for four comparative forms ending in -er. Circle or highlight them.

LANGUAGE LINK

Comparatives and Superlatives

Words with one or two syllables usually add -er and -est endings to form the comparative and the superlative.

light
lighter: Comparative
lightest: Superlative

Words with more than two syllables usually use the words *more* and *most*.

exciting
***more** exciting*: Comparative
***most** exciting*: Superlative

Refer to Grammar Book, Unit 7.

PRONUNCIATION

WORDS SPELLED WITH *EI*

The *ei* vowel combination is usually pronounced /ay/ as in *day*, but there are some exceptions.

Listen to these words and repeat each one after the speaker. Each word is paired with another word that has the same vowel sound.

Word Pairs

1. weight	**2.** neighbour	**3.** reign	**4.** beige	**5.** eight
way	navy	rain	bay	ate

Listen to these sentences. Underline all the vowel sounds that are the same as the vowel sound of the word in bold.

1. My neighbour can't wait to paint his gate **beige**.

2. People might lie about **height** on dating websites.

3. Lately, doctors are concerned about the fate of teenagers with an unhealthy **weight**.

4. Was King James' **reign** in Spain?

5. There were **eight** bagels on that plate. Who ate one?

Looks Can Be Deceiving

Lydia has to pick up two **couch-surfers** from the airport. She talks with them on the phone before the flight to **find out what they look like**.

VOCABULARY

Write the number of the picture that corresponds to each physical description word before you listen.

1. straight	**5.** a beard
2. curly	**6.** sideburns
3. freckles	**7.** tall
4. bald	**8.** short

Make sure you understand the definition of these words.

striped → marked with lines
a faux hawk → a hairstyle with a raised middle part

Listen to Natasha describe Peter and herself so that Bob and Lydia can recognize them. Help them by taking notes on their appearance.

Natasha

_____

_____

_____

_____

_____

Peter

_____

_____

_____

_____

_____

Answer the questions below.

1. Why do you think Natasha lied about her and Peter's appearance?

_____

_____

2. Draw Natasha and Peter using your notes. Compare your drawings with a partner.

Natasha

Peter

 WRITING

Describe Yourself!

Many websites require you to write a **description of yourself**. Can you recognize your **classmates** from their written descriptions? Can they recognize you from yours? What if you only changed one fact? Could you still **recognize** each other?

Write your personal profile for a social networking website. Write one paragraph to describe yourself (height, hair colour, etc.). Use adjectives, comparatives, and the negative form. You can tell one "white lie" if you wish.

_____

_____

_____

_____

_____

_____

_____

 READING

Cheating at School

Is it **too easy** to cheat in school? Is cheating **worth the risk** just to get better marks? In this text, students give their opinions on the **problem of cheating** in higher education.

VOCABULARY

Circle the correct definition of the words in bold before you read.

1. **Faking** a doctor's note is a serious offence.   a. providing   b. falsifying
2. Some students cheat on a **daily** basis.   a. often   b. every day
3. The **penalty** for cheating is not serious enough.   a. reason   b. consequence
4. The issue of cheating must be **dealt with**.   a. resolved   b. ignored
5. The consequences are a real **threat**.   a. possible danger   b. reason to continue
6. He got a good **mark** on his presentation, 85%!   a. note   b. result
7. Her exam results **barely** surprised her.   a. not very much   b. very much

Read the text below.

Research Suggests Many Students Cheat, Young People Concur

By Noor Javed
Canadian Press

On most campuses in Canada, final exams are the most stressful time of the year. Students preparing for exams at the University of Toronto said their opinions on cheating depend on how we define cheating.

"I wouldn't even consider cheating during an exam," said Justine King, a first-year social sciences student at the University of Toronto.

"I've thought of ways, but I haven't done it yet... Maybe next year when I'm in second year?" she added **laughingly**.

But for written assignments, the rules on cheating are a little more relaxed.

"I don't think helping each other on a lab, or doing an assignment in a group, is cheating," said Ionna Orphanides, a first-year science student.

"I don't even think **rewording** someone's assignment is a bad thing," she said.

Anecdotes like these are a major point of discussion in a study published in the Canadian *Journal of Higher Education* entitled "Academic Misconduct within Higher Education in Canada."

The study, co-authored by Professor Julia Christensen Hughes, chair of the Department of Business at the University of Guelph, and Donald McCabe of Rutgers University, found that 53 per cent of nearly 15,000 Canadian **undergraduate students** admitted to cheating on written work at least once in the 12 months before the survey.

"I think our results are fairly consistent with research done in other countries," said Hughes, who is also the president of the Society for Teaching and Learning in Higher Education.

Part of the problem, Hughes said, is a lack of consistency on how the issue is dealt with.

"Many students feel there is little risk in getting caught," she said. "And even if they are caught, the penalties aren't necessarily that serious."

"I've heard of stolen exams, tests, quizzes, people texting each other answers, or writing things on their legs and hands," said Katie Davis, a third-year student. "It's not anything new."

"In my exam today, a girl was looking over someone's shoulder, but she wasn't penalized," said Asma Hussein, who was preparing for a biology lab. "They just moved her to the front of the exam hall."

Stories like these are familiar to academic officers on campuses who deal with cheating on a daily basis. The University of Windsor is one of the many universities that list academic discipline cases on a website.

Some of the instances listed include "serious" exam cheating, like faking a doctor's note, taking a cheat sheet into the exam room, or even **impersonation** cases, said Danielle Istl, the academic integrity officer at the University of Windsor.

"The study isn't trying to say all students are cheaters," she said. "It's more like this is a complex issue that we need to understand and need to look at what students, faculty, and administrators need to do to create cultures of integrity on campus."

"In our opinion, we think it barely affects the university if we cheat and get a better mark," said Orphanides.

"I think if universities and professors really cared about our cheating, they would give us assignments that were more individualized, and quizzes administered with **TAs** watching and not online quizzes," said Kristin Mcilroy, a third-year science student.

"So I think they know that students are cheating in some cases."

And for some, the fear of the consequences that may come as a result are not enough of a threat.

"Even if there is fear of getting caught, the fear of failing a course is so much greater that sometimes you are willing to take the risk," said Orphanides. "It's not that difficult of a decision to make."

laughingly → with a laugh

impersonation → pretending to be someone else

rewording → changing the words

undergraduate students → university students working towards a bachelor's degree

TAs → teaching assistants

6. What are the most common reasons students cheat? Complete the chart.

Reasons for Cheating	Answers
a. Most common reason	
b. Second most common reason	
c. Third most common reason	

7. What do you think schools should do to prevent cheating?

_____

_____

_____

Procedures for Project 3, The Citizenship Game (page 94)

"Married" Couple

1. Work with the other spouse on your team.
2. Read the interview topics and find out as much as you can about your spouse.
3. The citizenship judges will interview you separately. No notes are permitted.
4. Convince the citizenship judges that you love each other and prove that your marriage is genuine. You may have to lie.

Citizenship Judges

1. Work with the other judge on your team.
2. Read the interview topics and prepare ten questions to ask the "married" couple. One of you will interview the "husband" and the other will interview the "wife". Make sure you plan your questions so that you can compare if the answers are the same. For example, one of you asks the "wife" about her habits, and the other asks the "husband" about his "wife's" habits.
3. Decide who will interview which spouse. You will interview the couple separately and write down the answers.
4. When finished, compare the answers and count the number of mistakes. More than 3 mistakes means no citizenship!

Possible Interview Topics

- Details of the wedding and honeymoon (such as when, where, guests, weather, duration)

- Physical descriptions (such as age, eye colour, birthmarks)

- Details on how and when the couple met, first date, etc.

- Favourite things (such as food, movie, colour)

- Habits and routines

- Past vacations and outings

WRITING FILES

Topic Sentences and Supporting Details

How do I support my topic sentence?

Support your topic sentence with examples, facts, statistics, or anecdotes. Supporting details should give relevant information but should not go off topic or be repetitive.

Read the topic sentence below and draw a line through the supporting details that do not relate to the topic sentence.

Topic sentence: Many people think that they won't get caught lying on their CVs.

Supporting details:

1. Companies hire CV detectives to check if a candidate lied on their CV.
2. Many companies only accept online CVs.
3. Some people really want the job and will do anything, including lying, to get it.
4. People lie on dating websites too.
5. More men than women lie on their CV.
6. Most lies are exaggerations about qualifications and experience.
7. It is important for the company to find the right employee.
8. A CV should include academic information and work experience.

Read the paragraph below. Circle the topic sentence and underline the supporting details.

Students can avoid unintentional plagiarism by careful planning and by having some knowledge about what plagiarism is. Remember that using someone's words as your own without citing the source is plagiarism. Some examples of plagiarism include copying a friend's homework or lab report. Be careful when you research and use information from the Internet because someone else wrote that work, too! To avoid plagiarism, you can paraphrase or rewrite the ideas from the text in your own words, include a direct quote using quotations marks, or mention the source in an indirect quote. Here is an example of an indirect quote about the text on page 89: Hughes says that the problem with cheating is that students do not feel they will get caught.

Write a paragraph for one of these topic sentences. Include supporting details.

   a. It is acceptable to tell a "white lie" if no one gets hurt.
   b. There are many ways to tell if someone is lying.
   c. Letting someone help you on an assignment is/isn't cheating.
   d. Schools need better rules and more consequences to prevent cheating.

Project 1

A Questionnaire

Prepare a questionnaire about lying or cheating on one of these topics:

Friendship   Technology   School   Parents
Work   Driving   Dating   Shopping

1. Write five questions. Refer to the Warm-Up, page 78 for a model of a questionnaire.
2. Interview at least five students.
3. Highlight essential information from your notes.
4. Summarize your results in a paragraph.
5. Present your results to the class.
6. Use comparatives and superlatives.

*Most people thought that taking something from work was **less serious than** stealing from a store.*

 Project 2

A Personal Ad

You want to help your best friend get a date with a classmate. Describe your best friend in a paragraph.

1. Describe your best friend using the third-person singular form of the simple present.
2. Write at least ten descriptions.
3. Include negative forms and comparatives.

 Project 3

The Citizenship Game

The object of the game is to correctly answer the citizenship judge's questions and obtain Canadian citizenship. You will role-play either a spouse or citizenship judge.

1. Form teams of four. Decide who will be the "married" couple and who will be the two citizenship judges.
2. Read the instructions on page 92 for your role.
3. Refer to page 92 for the list of possible interview topics.
4. Conduct the interview and find out who gets citizenship.

Top Words

Put a check mark next to the words you know. Learn the words you do not remember.

- [ ] behaviour
- [ ] a clue
- [ ] daily
- [ ] to figure out
- [ ] honest
- [ ] integrity*
- [ ] least
- [ ] to lie
- [ ] proof
- [ ] a trait

Review, Recycle, Remember

Incorporate the following items into your project files where appropriate.

- Comparative and superlative forms
- Vocabulary and *In Words* from the unit
- Highlighting essential information
- Talking about perceptions
- Supporting your topic sentence
- Topic sentences and supporting details

What Is Your
INSPIRATION?

Talented, innovative, and YOUNG

Who are your role models?

Is today's generation too narcissistic?

How does music inspire young people?

In this unit, you will explore how young people can make a difference, no matter what challenges they face.

UNIT 6

AGAINST ALL ODDS

 WARM-UP

Who Is Your Role Model?

Which famous people or celebrities make great **role models**? Do you admire *politicians or pop singers*? Who inspires you? Who does not?

Write the names of positive and negative role models for each of the categories in the chart below. Give the reason for your choices. Refer to the box in the margin for some additional ideas.

Category	Positive Role Model	Reason	Negative Role Model	Reason
1. Athlete				
2. Actor				
3. Musician				
4. Other				

Possible Role Models
doctor or nurse
environmentalist
foreign-aid worker
humanitarian
scientist
spiritual leader

Compare your chart in small groups. Select the winners of the "Best Role Model of the Year" and "Worst Role Model of the Year" awards. Support your decision with an example of why this person is a positive or negative role model.

Best Role Model of the Year	Worst Role Model of the Year

How to...

Emphasize Your Point

Add information to support your statement by using these words or phrases: *actually, as a matter of fact, also, in fact.*

Christopher Reeves was a great actor; **in fact***, he was an even greater role model after he became paraplegic.*

DISCUSSION

1. Do celebrities use their fame to make a difference? Explain.
2. How can an ordinary person make a difference?
3. What can young people do to have an impact on the world around them?

Generation Who?

Jean Twenge, a psychology professor, conducted research on **today's generation** of young people, which she calls "Generation Me." Do you agree or disagree that young people today are **too narcissistic**?

VOCABULARY

Match each word or expression with its correct definition before you read. The line number is in parentheses.

1. self-centred (2)	**a.** consistently
2. a trend (5)	**b.** a tendency
3. endlessly (7)	**c.** without stopping
4. steadily (24)	**d.** heat
5. warmth (39)	**e.** untruthfulness
6. dishonesty (40)	**f.** selfish
7. to react (46)	**g.** to respond to a situation

Complete the chart by writing the correct forms of the words provided.

Noun	Adjective	Adverb
1. warmth	warm	
2. end		endlessly
3. steadiness	steady	

LANGUAGE LINK

Adverbs

Adverbs explain how something is done. They also modify an adjective.

*The fundraiser was **really** successful.* (describes *how* successful the fundraiser was)

To form adverbs, you usually add *-ly* to an adjective.

*quick → quick**ly**
endless → endless**ly***

Note: The adverb form of *good* is *well*.

*She speaks English **well**.*

Refer to Grammar Book, Unit 7.

Read the text.

University Students Think They're *So* Special

Study finds alarming rise in narcissism, self-centredness in "Generation Me"

Associated Press

Today's university students are more **narcissistic** and self-centred than their **predecessors**, according to a new study by five psychologists
5 who worry that the trend could be harmful to personal relationships and society.

"We need to stop endlessly repeating 'You're **special**' and having children repeat that back," said the study's lead author,
10 Professor Jean Twenge of San Diego State University. "Kids are self-centred enough already."

Twenge and her colleagues examined the responses of 16,475 college students nation-

narcissistic → obsessed with oneself

predecessors → people from a previous generation

special → wonderful, unique

breakdown → when
something falls apart

short-lived → for a very
short time

lack → not have

15 wide who completed an evaluation called the Narcissistic Personality Inventory (NPI) between 1982 and 2006.

The standardized inventory asks for responses to such statements as "If I ruled the 20 world, it would be a better place," "I think I am a special person," and "I can live my life any way I want to."

The researchers say students' NPI scores have risen steadily since the current test was 25 introduced in 1982. By 2006, they said, two-thirds of the students had above-average scores, 30 per cent more than in 1982.

We're all above average!

Narcissism can have benefits, said study co-30 author W. Keith Campbell of the University of Georgia, suggesting it could be useful in meeting new people "or auditioning on *American Idol*."

"Unfortunately, narcissism can also have very negative consequences for society, including 35 the **breakdown** of close relationships with others," he said.

The study says that narcissists "are more likely to have romantic relationships that are **short-lived**, at risk for infidelity, **lack** emotional warmth, 40 and to exhibit game-playing, dishonesty, and over-controlling and violent behaviours."

Twenge, the author of *Generation Me: Why Today's Young Americans Are More Confident, Assertive, Entitled—and More Miserable Than* 45 *Ever Before*, said narcissists tend to lack empathy, react aggressively to criticism, and favour self-promotion over helping others.

The researchers traced the phenomenon back to the promotion of high **self-esteem** in 50 the 1980s, asserting that the effort to build self-confidence had gone too far.

self-esteem → self-worth
or confidence

Answer the questions below.

1. What is the main idea of the text? Circle the correct answer.
   a. We're all above average!
   b. Narcissism could be harmful to personal relationships and society.
   c. College students are becoming more self-centred.
   d. Jean Twenge is the author of the book *Generation Me*.

2. Why is being a narcissist a problem in society? Circle all the correct answers.
   a. It can cause the breakdown of close relationships.
   b. Narcissists may cheat and have shorter romantic relationships.
   c. Narcissists may show more emotional warmth.
   d. Narcissists may be more dishonest and aggressive.

3. What are some benefits of narcissism?

_____

4. What does the author recommend we do to prevent our children from becoming narcissistic?

_____

_____

5. What does the author think caused this growing trend?

_____

_____

6. Do you agree or disagree with Twenge?

_____

_____

Write Back! A Response Letter

Do you **agree** or **disagree** with Professor Jean Twenge? Do you think **today's young people** are more narcissistic and self-centred than in the past? What would you like to tell her?

Write her a letter explaining your point of view. Support your statements with examples.

Address

Date

Dear_____ ,

_____

_____

_____

_____

Sincerely,

How to...

Write a Letter

Refer to the Writing Files, page 112.

FYI

The word *narcissism*, or self-love, comes from the ancient story of a handsome Greek who fell in love with his own reflection in a pool. Eventually, he was changed by the goddess Nemesis into a flower, the narcissus.

LISTENING

Who Is Eligible?

Samantha wants to **apply as a candidate** for the Top 20 Under 20™ awards program. This Canadian program awards inspiring people **under the age of 20**. Find out if she is eligible!

Part 1: Question Forms

Listen to Samantha's answers. What were the interview questions? Write an interview question for each of her answers.

 What are you studying?

1. _____   5. _____

2. _____   6. _____

3. _____   7. _____

4. _____   8. _____

Part 2: Sort the Information

Scan the information on Youth in Motion's Top 20 under 20™ awards program. Put a check mark in either the Eligibility Requirements or Awards Information column.

	Eligibility Requirements	Awards Information
1. Is under the age of 20 (as of December of the year they are applying)	✓	
2. Will receive up to $5,000 to be used for an educational experience		
3. Will have training in leadership development		
4. Demonstrated innovation, leadership, and achievement in his or her community		
5. Is not a past recipient of the Top 20 Under 20™ Award		
6. Has a desire to continue education or training in a Canadian high school, college, university, or apprenticeship program		
7. Will be recognized as a Top 20 Under 20™ winner in the media		
8. Will travel to Toronto for the Top 20 Under 20™ ceremony, all expenses paid		
9. Has Canadian citizenship or landed immigrant status		

Part 3: Can Samantha Apply?

Determine if Samantha can apply for the Top 20 Under 20™ award, using the information you heard and read.

Circle the correct answer and then explain why she is or is not eligible.

Samantha (is / isn't) eligible because

_____

_____

 LISTENING

Music Therapy

Listen to an interview from CBC: *Sounds Like Canada* with Raymond Ko, a young man who **won an award** for **his use of music**.

Make sure you understand the definitions of these words before you listen.

gifted → exceptionally talented

to hinder → to prevent, harm or make an action difficult to achieve

Listen to the interview and answer the questions below.

1. What is the main idea of the interview? Circle the correct answer.

    a. Raymond Ko talks about his community work with autistic children.

    b. Autistic children can improve through exposure to music.

    c. The Top 20 Under 20™ award winners are exceptional people.

2. What is Raymond Ko studying? _____

3. Why is Raymond in Belize? Circle the correct answer.

    a. He is learning about the tropical rain forest and how to conserve it.

    b. He is there to relax and enjoy the Caribbean Sea.

    c. Both a and b are correct.

4. What aspect of Raymond Ko's work caught the attention of the judges?

_____

_____

5. How is he a unique winner? What is different about him?

_____

_____

6. Where is his community? Circle the correct answer.

    a. Belize   **b.** Saskatoon   **c.** Saskatchewan   **d.** Manitoba

7. Which statements about Raymond's involvement with music are true? Put a check mark in the T or F to indicate if the statement is *true* or *false*.

	T	F
a. His older brothers and sisters, and parents all encouraged him.		
b. He studied violin, cello, and piano and received diplomas at age 15.		
c. He won at the National Music Festival in 2005.		

8. Who does Raymond's music therapy program help?

_____

9. According to Raymond's definition, what does autism affect? Circle all the correct answers.

    a. communication   **b.** sensations   **c.** emotions   **d.** growth   **e.** behaviour

10. What does Raymond plan to do in ten years?

_____

Future

For possible future events or predictions, use *will* or *be going to.*

He **will** probably **give** all the money to charity. (possible future event)

We **are going** to be very famous one day. (prediction)

For planned or definite future events, use *be going to.*

What **are** you **going to do** with the award money? (planned future event)

Note: The contraction of *will not* is *won't.*

He **won't apply** for the award this year.

Refer to Grammar Book, Unit 8.

SPEAKING

The Award

Congratulations! You and your partner won the **$5,000** "Most Innovative Youth Award" for your great ideas!

Discuss your future plans or predictions for the award money with your partner.

Write five sentences explaining what you and your partner will do with the money.

*My partner **is going to go** on a responsible travel tour of India.*

READING

Against the Odds

These **two young people** are making an **impact** on the world around them. Find out how!

Part 1: Pair Reading

Find a partner. Decide who will read the biography of Jordin Tootoo, and who will read the biography of Justin Hines.

Read the biography you selected. Do the vocabulary section and answer the questions that follow the text. In Part 2, you will exchange vocabulary words with your partner and share information to complete a chart.

Jordin Tootoo Coming in First

Jordin Tootoo was the first **Inuk** to be drafted into the National Hockey League. He was also chosen as captain for Team Canada under–18 at a tournament in
5 Europe. In 2002, he was awarded the National Aboriginal Achievement Award for youth for his athletic accomplishments.

Tootoo was born Jordin John *Kudluk* ("thunder") Tootoo on February 2, 1983, in Manitoba.
10 He grew up in Rankin Inlet, which is a city in Nunavut, Canada's newest territory. His mother is of Ukrainian-Canadian descent, and his father is an Inuk from Nunavut. Jordin started skating before the age of three.

15 It was a challenge to train and practise in an isolated Northern community. In the Arctic, the cost of living is high and resources are very limited. To weight train, Jordin had to lift not only cans of food, but also his cousin! Because the
20 terrain in the North is quite flat, Jordin needed to train indoors on special fitness equipment, like the Stairmaster.

Jordin currently plays for the Nashville Predators. Not surprisingly, his number is 22
25 (Tootoo). His older brother Terence also played hockey; sadly, he committed suicide at a young age. One of the reasons Jordin still plays hockey is to honour his brother.

Jordin knows what it means to be a role
30 model. He takes his role seriously. Jordin is the official spokesperson for two Northern companies, where he has the ability to inspire youth about the importance of staying in school, following their dreams, and achieving their goals.
35 He is also the owner of Team Tootoo, a sportswear company that makes clothing specifically designed for Arctic athletes.

Positive role models are really necessary in the harsh and isolated communities of the North.
40 When Jordin was growing up, he was inspired by another famous hockey player, Wendel Clark. Jordin says he always received support from his parents and family. He believes that with hard work and determination people can
45 achieve anything they put their hearts into.

Jordin has a vision: to be the best he can be and more. His personal goal is to win the Stanley Cup and bring it home to the Inuksuk, a towering stone monument at Rankin Inlet's
50 highest point.

Inuk → someone of Inuit origin

VOCABULARY

Define these words from the text. Use a dictionary if you need help. Define three other words from the text that you do not know.

New Words	Definitions		Words of Your Choice	Definitions
1. to weight train (18)			4.	
2. a spokesperson (31)			5.	
3. harsh (39)			6.	

Answer the questions below.

1. Why was it such an accomplishment for Jordin to play professional hockey? Circle the correct answer.

    a. The Inuit people don't play hockey.   **c.** It was too cold in Rankin Inlet.

    b. His family did not have enough money.   **d.** Resources are limited in the North.

2. What else does Jordin do besides play hockey? Circle T or F to indicate if the statement is *true* or *false*. If it is *false*, write the correct statement on the line provided.

    a. He is a spokesperson.   T   F

    _____

    b. He designs clothes for Arctic athletes.   T   F

    _____

    c. He helps inspire youth to achieve their goals.   T   F

    _____

    d. He owns two Northern companies.   T   F

    _____

3. Underline four adverbs in the text that end in *-ly*. Write them below.

_____

A Story of Inspiration

Justin Hines says he doesn't remember wanting anything else besides a career in music. The young singer-song-writer's debut album *Sides* features the
5 song "Wish You Well," which he sang for the Walk for Miracles campaign, in support of The Hospital for Sick Children in Toronto. His music is often about how he sees life positively, about finding beauty "in life's darkest situations," and
10 about providing comfort for the soul.

Justin's talent was noticed early on. As a baby, he could easily carry a tune even before he was able to speak. It helped that he has a musical family. His father plays the folk guitar. His grand-
15 mother also encouraged him to sing. When he was 14 years old, Justin won a radio contest to sing the Canadian national anthem in front of 17,000 people at a Toronto Raptors game.

What makes this young man's journey
20 absolutely amazing is that he suffers from a rare condition called Larsen syndrome. This condition severely affects the joints in the body. As a result, he is confined to a wheel-chair, but he remains positive. He even has a
25 mantra: look for hope to shine through in all things, regardless of the circumstances.

"My theory," says Justin "is that if you truly analyze your life, there is never a shortage of inspiration." His sources of inspiration were
30 artists such as James Taylor, Willie Nelson, Cat Stevens, and Jim Croce. He used to listen to them on his dad's jukebox.

Justin has a selfless love for humanity. He started performing for charitable events and
35 fundraisers as young as age ten. Justin Hines says he simply wants to help others by giving. He also gets to combine a passion for music with his desire to spread the message of love. He believes that it is his duty to give back to the
40 earth as much as he has taken.

Define these words from the text. Use a dictionary if you need help. Define three other words from the text that you do not know.

New Words	Definitions		Words of Your Choice	Definitions
1. a folk guitar (14)		**4.**		
2. an anthem (17)		**5.**		
3. a mantra (25)		**6.**		

Answer the questions below.

1. What makes Justin's music career so special?

_____

_____

2. What else do you know about Justin? Circle T or F to indicate if the statement is *true* or *false*. If it is *false*, write the correct statement on the line provided.

a. He sang the American national anthem in front of 17,000 people. T F

_____

b. His music is about the sadness of life's darkest situations. T F

_____

c. He believes there are many sources of inspiration. T F

_____

d. He is involved with charities and fundraisers. T F

_____

3. Underline four adverbs in the text that end in *-ly*. Write them below.

_____

Part 2: Reading Retell

Share the six words and definitions from your vocabulary section with a partner. Write your partner's words and definitions in the vocabulary chart found on either page 103 or 105.

Project 1

Role Model of the Year
Write a letter recommending your role model for an award. You may select someone from the Warm-Up on page 96.

1. Give general background information about your role model.
2. Explain why you recommend this person.
3. Write briefly about the role model's accomplishments.
4. Support your statements.
5. Include your address and the date.

 Project 2

The Song Project
Present a song which touches or inspires you.

1. Select an inspiring English-language song and interpret the general meaning of the song's lyrics.
2. Search for biographical information on the artist or group.
3. Present a short biography of the artist or group.
4. Explain the general meaning of the song.
5. Play a short segment of the song.

 Project 3

Your Inspiration Interview
Think of someone you admire to interview, either a family member, a friend, or even someone who works in a field you are interested in.

1. Ask five questions and be prepared to record the answers.
2. Use the correct verb tenses.
3. Make sure to include a question about the future.
4. In small groups, present what you learned and how this inspires you.

Top Words

Put a check mark next to the words you know and learn the ones you do not remember.

- [ ] to attend
- [ ] fortunate
- [ ] a goal*
- [ ] to raise
- [ ] to react*
- [ ] rest
- [ ] self-centred
- [ ] steadily
- [ ] a trend*
- [ ] unknown

Review, Recycle, Remember

Incorporate the following items into your project files where appropriate.

- ■ Future
- ■ Adverbs
- ■ Vocabulary and *In Words* from the unit
- ■ Asking for clarification
- ■ Emphasizing a point
- ■ Interpreting a message
- ■ Letter writing

Examining Health
MYTHS

Healthy choices for you and the ENVIRONMENT

What do you believe about some popular health myths?

What health challenges do students face?

What is the 100-mile diet and how can it help the environment?

In this unit, you will look at how making healthy changes can impact your world.

UNIT 7

FOOD FOR THOUGHT

 WARM-UP

Health Check

Sometimes **students** get too busy with their studies and neglect their **health**. Are you living a **balanced lifestyle**?

Read the health questionnaire and fill in the missing auxiliary or verb in the blank spaces. Write two more questions about health habits.

Complete the questionnaire and record your answers in the first column. Then interview your classmates. Write the names of students who have the closest answers to yours.

How to...

Agree or Disagree with Someone

To agree with someone's affirmative statement, use:

me too, so do I, I also...

*Yes, **so do I**. **I also** eat cereal for breakfast.*

To agree with someone's negative statement, use:

me neither, ...either.

*I don't work **either**.*

Health Questions	Your Response	Student's Name
1. _____ you eat breakfast everyday?		
What _____ you usually eat?		
2. How many hours of sleep _____ you get every night?		
3. How many hours a week _____ you work?		
4. How often _____ you exercise?		
5. _____ you procrastinate or finish your work on time?		
6. _____ you eat fruits and vegetables every day?		
7. What _____ your favourite junk food?		
8. _____ you buy local food, or food that is imported?		
9. Your question:		
10. Your question:		

DISCUSSION

1. What are some health issues that students face?
2. What changes do you want to make for a healthier lifestyle?

Myth or Advice?

Myth: You can catch a cold by going outside with wet hair.
What other **advice** have your parents or **grandparents** told you? Is this advice always true? Find out what is really a **myth** and what is really **good advice**!

VOCABULARY

Match each word or expression with its correct definition before you read. The line number is in parentheses.

1. to contain (7)	**a.**	an illness that causes a runny nose, sneezing, etc.
2. a cold or flu (18)	**b.**	a false belief, legend
3. to soothe (19)	**c.**	to have within or include
4. sore (20)	**d.**	to comfort
5. to ease (22)	**e.**	cold
6. a cough (23)	**f.**	air expelled from the lungs with force
7. chilly (30)	**g.**	painful
8. a myth (33)	**h.**	a digestive organ
9. a stomach (39)	**i.**	to make easier
10. wealthy (53)	**j.**	rich

Read the text.

Common Health Myths

Here is some health advice that you might remember hearing your own grandmother tell you. Is it all a myth?

1. An apple a day keeps the doctor away.
5 Can apples really keep you in good health? In fact, apples, like any fruit, are good for you. Apples contain antioxidants which **ward off** cancer and heart disease. They also contain pectin, a fibre which helps eliminate the body's
10 cholesterol. Overall, apples contain less nutrients and vitamins than berries or oranges. One slice of potato has as much vitamin C as an apple. Although they may not keep the doctor away, they can certainly help.

15 **2. You should eat chicken soup when you have a cold.**
Well, Grandma was right, eating chicken soup might help you feel better during a cold or flu. Soup keeps the body hydrated and soothes a
20 sore throat. Some scientific studies concluded that chicken soup contains an anti-inflammatory agent that eases cold symptoms like a stuffy nose, a cough, and a sore throat.

3. You can catch a cold by going outside
25 **with wet hair.**
Can you really get sick by going outside in the cold with wet hair? No, you cannot. Bacteria and viruses can cause a cold or the flu, not wet hair in cold weather. The worst that will happen
30 is that you will feel chilly.

ward off → prevent

4. Do not crack your knuckles or you might get arthritis.

This is just another myth. Cracking knuckles does not cause arthritis. The popping sound you
35 hear is an air bubble that forms in the joint fluid when you pull them. As a matter of fact, arthritis has several causes, including genetic factors, age, and injury, for example.

**5. You must not swim on a full stomach; you
40 should wait at least an hour.**

It's healthy to wait a little a bit before swimming, but you do not have to wait an entire hour. Some professional athletes often eat right before training or competing.

45 **6. You shouldn't read in dim light.**

Reading in dim light might make the eyes tired but it certainly does not result in a need for glasses, and neither does sitting too close to the TV. And yes, eat those carrots; they contain
50 vitamin A, which is good for the eyes. Do you see any rabbits wearing glasses?

7. Early to bed and early to rise makes a man healthy, wealthy, and wise.

Benjamin Franklin made this saying popular for
55 good reason. No one can disagree with the

health benefits of sleep. Many studies show that if you do not get enough sleep, you could end up with poor health.

**8. You should never swallow gum, it takes
60 seven years to digest.**

Your stomach is quite capable of handling a piece of gum. Any gum you swallow passes through your system within 24 hours. It will not stick to your insides. And no, a watermelon seed
65 will not grow into a watermelon inside your stomach. It is just another myth!

9. Eating chocolate can cause acne.

Aren't you glad that this one is not true? Acne has many causes, such as stress, genetics, skin type,
70 and hormones. Go ahead and eat that chocolate!

10. The toilet seat has the most germs in a public bathroom.

Your computer keyboard, mouse, phone, and the top of your desk are covered with many
75 more germs than a toilet seat. In fact, studies show that the floor is one of the dirtiest places in a public bathroom. However, if you want to choose a place with the least amount of germs, use the first stall in a public bathroom because
80 most people use the ones in the back.

Answer the questions below.

1. What is the main idea of the text? Circle the correct answer.
   a. All the health advice our grandmothers gave us was made up of myths.
   b. Health myths may or may not contain some truth.
   c. You should live reasonably to stay healthy.
   d. An apple a day keeps the doctor away.

2. Which statement is *false*? Circle the correct answer.
   a. Chicken soup helps you feel better during a cold or flu.
   b. Going out with wet hair can make you catch a cold.
   c. You don't have to wait an hour after you eat to go swimming.
   d. Arthritis is not caused by cracking your knuckles.

3. What does the text recommend for good eye health?

   _____

4. Explain the statement Benjamin Franklin made popular, in your own words.

   _____

   _____

5. How long does the stomach need to digest a piece of gum?

_____

6. What causes acne, according to the text? Circle all the correct answers.

a. eating chocolate   **b.** genetics   **c.** stress   **d.** skin type

7. Is a toilet seat is one of the dirtiest places in a bathroom? Explain.

_____

DISCUSSION

1. What are some other health myths that you know about?
2. Who told you this myth?
3. Do you think it is true? Explain.

PRONUNCIATION

/TH/ SOUND

The /th/ sound found in words like _health_, _think_, and _with_ can be tricky to pronounce. Make sure to differentiate this sound from the /t/ sound. Try to stick out your tongue when you say /th/.

Listen to the recording and fill in the blanks with the words you hear. Then, read the complete sentences with a partner to compare your answers and to practise saying the /th/ sound.

1. Students should _____ about changes to their lifestyle.

2. They should not eat _____ or sugary foods which can ruin their

_____ .

3. _____ sleep and exercise are also shown to improve class performance.

4. Our grandparents also _____ about _____ eating.

5. Our parents _____ us to make wise choices.

6. Food grown on _____ is good for you.

7. _____ people tried the diet. Now they're _____ .

8. You should try green _____ .

9. _____ you for helping me _____ my work.

10. I will talk to you at _____ o'clock.

Repeat these tongue twisters as fast as you can. Work with a partner.

1. Tom thought he brought with him the thin broth he bought from Buddy, but he forgot.
2. Did Tim think of thanking both Beth and Todd for the thoughtful tin of tea?
3. I thought a thought. But the thought I thought wasn't the thought I thought I thought.

IN WORDS

The Verb *Get*

The verb *get* is used together with certain words to express different meanings. Many of these expressions are related to health, fitness, and lifestyle choices.

Read ten different uses of the verb *get*.

1. **to get into shape** → to train or exercise
2. **to get some sleep/rest** → to go to bed and sleep/rest
3. **to get something/lunch/supper** → to retrieve or buy something/lunch/supper
4. **to get up** → to wake up and start the day
5. **to get sick** → to become ill
6. **to get engaged/married/divorced** → to become a fiancé/someone's spouse/to end a marriage
7. **to get into trouble** → to be in a bad situation
8. **to get to** (a place) → to arrive at a destination
9. **to get better** → to not be sick; to improve
10. **to get ready** → to prepare

Complete each sentence with an expression from the list above.

1. Jessie hopes she can __get_____ her gym membership soon, so she can _____ really good _____.

2. I hope you can _____ more _____ tomorrow night. Insomnia is not good for you!

3. Franco has to _____ every morning at 5:00 a.m. He has to work quite early.

4. Susan might go to the cafeteria to _____. It is almost noon and she is hungry.

5. She will _____ if she takes her medicine.

6. Be careful not to _____, or you may disappoint your parents.

7. Tina has to _____ to leave. Her friend will pick her up in ten minutes.

8. You could _____ if you don't wash your hands often. There are a lot of germs!

9. How can we _____ the farmer's market? I forgot the directions.

10. My sister will _____ next summer. She bought her wedding dress.

Sleepless in College

Myth: Pulling all-nighters is okay to study for an exam.

How much **sleep** do you really need and how can you get a better night's **rest**? Find out what the experts advise.

VOCABULARY

Circle the correct definition for each word in bold below before you read.

1. I **require** more sleep.	**a.** need	**b.** ask for
2. You feel **alert**.	**a.** in danger	**b.** awake and ready
3. It can **interfere** with school.	**a.** help with	**b.** cause problems
4. **Recall** the information.	**a.** phone again	**b.** remember
5. It can **decrease** functions.	**a.** describe	**b.** reduce
6. It can **weaken** the immune system.	**a.** lower its strength	**b.** make it stronger

Match each word or expression in bold with its correct definition before you read. The line number is in parentheses.

1. It might **lower** the results. (36)	**a.** how you feel
2. Your **mood** could change. (37)	**b.** negatively affect
3. This may **impair** your ability to drive. (50)	**c.** a preoccupation
4. You should slow your **pace**. (59)	**d.** a short period of sleep
5. It's **on your mind**. (62)	**e.** reduce
6. She has to take a **nap**. (73)	**f.** speed or rhythm

Read the text.

Sleep

Brown University

sleep-deprived → unable to get enough sleep

irregularity → inconsistency

REM → dream sleep (Rapid Eye Movement

occasional → rarely occurring

College students are among the most **sleep-deprived** people in the country. This may be due to the **irregularity** of their sleeping habits. According to a 5 study, only 11% of college students have good sleep quality, and 73% have **occasional** sleep problems. This same study found that 18% of college men and 30% of college women reported suffering from insomnia within the past three 10 months, and over half reported feeling sleepy during the morning.

Most people need to sleep about eight hours each night. This is especially true for college students, since the deep sleep that occurs early in 15 the night and the dream sleep that occurs later in the night are both required to learn. But the necessary amount of sleep varies from individual to individual. This is one case where quality is more important than quantity – if you feel alert 20 and rested during the day, you've probably gotten enough sleep.

On the other hand, **pulling all-nighters** can interfere with your ability to learn new material. You can memorize facts during an all-night study 25 session and recall the information through short-term memory for a test the next day, but you will most likely have to re-learn the material for a later cumulative exam.

drowsy → sleepy

pulling all-nighters → staying up all night

enhances → improves

sleep debts → number of hours of sleep lost

slump → sudden decline in energy

What happens if I don't get enough sleep?

30 **Sleep debts** result from not getting enough sleep for several nights. Building up your sleep debt results in a decrease in daytime function. It can affect your physical health by weakening your immune system. It can affect your mental 35 health by resulting in tension, irritability, depression, confusion, and it generally lowers life satisfaction. These mood changes may also result from irregular sleeping patterns, including sleeping in on the weekends.

40 It is well documented that sleep deprived students perform significantly worse than students who regularly get a good night's sleep. REM sleep is particularly important for consolidating newly learned information, and a large propor- 45 tion of REM sleep occurs towards the end of the night. So studying most of the night for a test, and then sleeping only a few hours, decreases your ability to remember new information.

Not getting enough sleep also seriously 50 impairs your ability to drive. Driving while tired is as dangerous as driving while intoxicated - more than 40,000 injuries and 1,500 deaths each year result from traffic accidents involving sleepy drivers.

55 **How can I get a better night's sleep?**

Here are a few things you can do to make falling asleep easier and to make sleep more restful:

• Relax! An alert mind may make it difficult to sleep. Try to slow the pace of your activities in 60 the evening. Do some light reading or watch TV until you become **drowsy**, and then try to fall asleep naturally. If there's a lot on your mind, try writing down a detailed list and then forgetting about it.

65 • Avoid or limit caffeine and nicotine, which are stimulants, and alcohol, which can cause unrestful sleep and frequent awakenings during the night.

• Exercise and stay active. Twenty to thirty min- 70 utes of vigorous physical activity **enhances** deep sleep, but avoid exercising in the six hours before bedtime since it increases alertness.

• Avoid long naps. Naps of less than thirty minutes can actually be quite refreshing during 75 the naturally occurring mid-afternoon **slump** but napping for much longer than this can make you drowsy and interfere with a good night's sleep.

• Try to go to sleep and wake up at the same 80 time every day. A regular sleep pattern reduces insomnia, and increases your alertness during the day.

Answer the questions below.

1. Reflect on the reading. What is the main idea of the article? Circle the correct answer.

   a. Students need to sleep eight hours every night.

   b. Staying up all night can interfere with your ability to learn new material.

   c. College students have irregular sleep habits which affect their studies.

2. What two kinds of sleep are necessary for learning?

_____

3. Which statement is *not* a consequence of not sleeping enough, according to the text? Circle the correct answer.

   a. There is a decrease in daytime functioning.

   b. It can affect your physical health.

   c. It can cause weight loss.

   d. It might lower grades.

4. What does the article recommend for better sleep health? Complete the chart. Use modals in your answers.

Subject	Recommendations
a. Difficulty sleeping at night	You should try to relax, read, and fall asleep naturally.
b. Use of stimulants	
c. Exercise	
d. Naps	
e. Bedtime	

5. Write a question for each statement below, using the information in bold.

   a. Most people need to sleep **eight hours** each night.

   _____

   b. It can affect health **by weakening the immune system**.

   _____

   c. **Yes**, tired students perform significantly worse than students who regularly get a good night's sleep.

   _____

   _____

DISCUSSION

1. Do you agree with what the article says about sleep? Why or why not?
2. Do you think you practise good sleep habits?
3. What should you change to get more rest?

How to...

Reflect on Readings

Reflect on a reading by looking over the important information in the text. Try to connect the information from the text to other readings or your own personal experience.

As you read:

1. Ask yourself if the subject is familiar.

2. Have you read other texts or heard about the same subject? How is it similar?

3. Does it remind you of experiences from your own life?

Reflecting will help you to talk about the reading and provide your own insight.

LANGUAGE LINK

Modals

Use modals before verbs to make suggestions or recommendations.

*Students **should** plan their days better.*

*He **could** pack a lunch the night before.*

Note there is no –s after the main verb. (*could packs*)

Refer to Grammar Book, Unit 10.

FYI

A study shows that students who study late at night actually have lower grades than those who do not miss their sleep. You should get some rest and study during the daytime.

Solve the Riddle

Can you **guess the answer** to these riddles? **Make your own** for your classmates to solve!

Listen to the clues to the riddle and write down the modals that you hear. Solve the riddle and write the answer below.

Modals Riddle 1

1. You _____ do this in the summer.

2. You _____ want to do it in the forest.

3. You _____ want to do it alone or with friends.

4. You _____ go slowly the first time.

5. You _____ be careful if you have no experience.

6. You _____ do this without a horse.

Do you know what it is? _____.

Modals Riddle 2

1. You _____ do this regularly.

2. You _____ do this anywhere; you usually do it at home.

3. You _____ do this after a long day.

4. You _____ feel better after you do this.

5. People _____ wear special clothing for this.

6. You _____ try to do this for at least eight hours.

Do you know what it is? _____.

Create your own riddle for your classmates to solve on a separate sheet of paper.

1. In teams of two, select a health-related action verb, like "swim."
2. Write your riddle and include at least six clues.
3. Make sure clues begin with general descriptions that become more specific (so that no one can easily guess the answer after the first or second clue).
4. Use a different modal for each clue. Include one negative form.
5. Read your riddle to another team. Then try to solve their riddle.

Dear Angie

Sometimes you need to ask others for **advice**. Many newspapers publish **advice columns** where readers send in their questions about a **problem**. The advice columnists respond by giving advice.

Write a short letter for the "Dear Angie" advice column about a health-related problem that college students face. Use the ideas below to help you. Work in small groups.

alternative medicine	balancing work and studies	drug and alcohol use
failing courses	maintaining a social life	no time for exercise
poor diet	sleep problems	smoking
stress	weight loss	weight gain

1. Exchange your letter with another group and read the other group's letter.
2. Make suggestions using five different modals. Underline one negative modal.
3. Exchange letters with another group. Read their suggestions and then add your own.
4. Get back your original letter and read the suggestions.
5. Discuss the advice you received and choose the best suggestions.

● WATCHING

100-Mile Diet

Myth: All diets are just fads, and they don't work.

In this video, CBC News: *Sunday* challenges an **environmentally friendly** diet that uses only local food. Is it **practical** to follow and can you **lose weight**?

DISCUSSION

1. What do you usually eat for supper? What are the main ingredients you need?
2. Where do these ingredients come from? Which of these ingredients can be grown locally?

LANGUAGE LINK

Negative Modals

Add *not* after the modal to make it negative.

*You **should not** smoke.* (suggestion)

*We **must not** be late.* (obligation)

When *have to* is in the negative form, it is not an obligation, but an option.

*You **have to** eat healthy!* (obligation)

*You **don't have to** finish your plate, if you don't want to.* (option)

Refer to Grammar Book, Unit 10.

Use *at, on, until, along, in front of*, and *across from* for directions.

*Turn left **at** the stop sign.*

*Turn right **on** Wood Avenue.*

*Go straight **until** you reach the bakery.*

*Continue **along** Oak Street.*

*It's **at** the corner of Maple Road and Oak Street.*

*The bakery is **in front of** the bank.*

*The butcher is **across from** the deli.*

Student B

1. Start out at Bob the Butcher. Go straight along Atwater Avenue until you reach Brooke Street. Turn right and continue along Brooke Street until you reach Fort Street. Turn right. Pass Mason Street. Continue until you reach Catherine Street. Turn left. What is the second building on your right? _____

2. From Dan's Delicatessen, walk straight along Catherine Street. Turn right at Fort Street. Turn left on Mason Street. Turn right on Atwater Avenue. Continue until the end of the street. What is the last building on your left ? _____

3. From the church, go down Atwater Avenue. Turn right on Tupper Street. Turn right on Greene Avenue. Continue along Greene Avenue until you reach the parking lot. What place can you go to relax that is across from the parking lot? _____

LISTENING

Going Organic

Myth: Organic food is always better than regular food. Many people want to know if they are improving their health by going organic. This audio interview asks the question: Is buying organic products always the best option?

VOCABULARY

Circle the correct definition for each word below before you listen.

1. organic	a. unhealthy	b. grown in a natural manner
2. welfare	a. well-being	b. illness
3. to last	a. to remain fresh	b. to finish at the end
4. safety	a. security	b. danger
5. a scientist	a. a person who writes signs	b. a person who studies science
6. ripe	a. ready to eat	b. scratched or torn
7. an additive	a. a total amount	b. an extra substance added
8. to conduct	a. to produce	b. to do (research)

Listen to Sharon interview Stephen Barker, who works at Sunrise, an organic food store. She is trying to find out whether or not she should buy organic food.

Answer the questions below.

1. What is the main idea of the audio segment? Circle the correct answer.
   a. Organic food is better than regular food.
   b. There is no evidence that organic food is healthy for you.
   c. It is still difficult to determine if organic food is the healthier option.
   d. Organic food is more expensive than regular food.

2. What does Stephen say makes food organic?

   _____

3. Compare organic food with regular food by completing the chart below.

Qualities	Organic Food	Regular Food
a. How the food looks		
b. How long the food lasts		
c. Pesticide use		

4. According to Stephen, which factors affect food's nutrient levels? Circle the correct answers.
   a. where the food was grown
   b. the variety or type of food
   c. the colour and size of the food
   d. when the food was picked
   e. how long food was in a store

5. What advice did Stephen give about eating organic food? Circle the correct answer.
   a. You should buy fresh fruits and vegetables all year round.
   b. You should buy organic fruits and vegetables when the non-organic versions may have more pesticides (like apples and potatoes).
   c. You may want to grow food or raise chickens in your backyard.

6. Did Stephen help Sharon decide to try organic food? Why or why not?

   _____

   _____

   _____

   _____

WRITING FILES
Opinion Paragraphs

Express an Opinion

Do:
Use the following opinion statements to express your thoughts:

In my opinion,
I believe that, I don't think,
I am convinced that...

*I **strongly believe** that we should reduce our carbon footprint.*

Don't:
Use double pronouns.

Me, I think this diet works.

How do I write an effective opinion paragraph?
To write an effective opinion paragraph, follow the steps below.

1. Write a title for your paragraph.
2. Include a topic sentence.
3. Use opinion statements.
4. Support your opinions with examples and facts.
5. Finish your paragraph with a concluding statement using words such as *finally, to sum up,* or *to conclude.*

Read the opinion paragraph below.

Going Local

I read an article about author Barbara Kingsolver's experience with eating local food for one year with her family. It's described in her bestselling book, *Animal, Vegetable, Miracle: A Year of Food Life.* I am really interested in trying the 100-mile diet and eating only local food. I am convinced that eating only local food won't be easy because I just love non-local food like sushi. I am really going to miss ethnic food with its exotic spices, but I will try the 100-mile diet anyway. There are many farms in Quebec. Fresh produce, like tomatoes and corn, is also quite delicious, in my opinion. Last year I visited a Quebec ostrich farm. I think ostrich meat is tasty. It's low in fat, too. Finally, I believe that if I try the 100-mile diet, I might be able to lose weight while I am saving the planet.

Answer the questions below.

1. What is the topic sentence in this opinion paragraph?

_____

_____

2. How does the author support the statement, "I am convinced that eating only local food won't be easy"?

_____

_____

3. What are the opinion statements used in the text? Underline them.

4. Put a check mark in the Fact or Opinion column to indicate if the statement is *fact* or *opinion*.

	Fact	Opinion
a. *Animal, Vegetable, Miracle: A Year of Food Life* was a bestselling book.		
b. I think ostrich meat tastes delicious.		
c. There are many farms in Quebec.		
d. Fresh produce from a farm is quite delicious.		

5. Circle the concluding statement.

Write an opinion paragraph on one of the subjects below.

college students and health	health myths
buying organic food	the 100-mile diet

Project 1

Go Local!
What do you think of the 100-mile diet?

1. Try the 100-mile diet for one meal. Choose a recipe and modify it to use only local products. Make sure to check the labels when you go shopping!
2. Write an opinion paragraph about your experience. Support your opinion with examples. Your paragraph should answer the questions below.

   a. What was the easiest or most difficult part of your experience?
   b. What are your suggestions or recommendations?
   c. Do you want to try it again? Why or why not?

3. Include the recipe you tried.

 Project 2

The Green Project
You learned how the 100-mile diet reduces your carbon footprint. What else can you do?

1. Think about a green way to reduce carbon emissions at school, at work or at home. Refer to the list of ideas below.

   Buy biodegradable products
   Reduce water consumption
   Start a community compost
   Use public transport
   Use less electricity

2. Try doing it for one week and then present your experience to the class.
3. Make sure to use modals in your presentation whenever you give advice.

 Project 3

Myth Busters
Research some myths that interest you about the subject of health. You can choose a myth that you heard from your own family.

1. Research and present information that explains how the myth possibly started.
2. Provide a scientific explanation that proves or disproves the myth.
3. Give your opinion on the subject and ask your classmates what they believe about the myth.

Top Words

Put a check mark next to the words you know and learn the ones you do not remember.

- ☐ to contain
- ☐ to decrease
- ☐ a feast
- ☐ to last
- ☐ to lower
- ☐ a myth
- ☐ organic
- ☐ to require*
- ☐ ripe
- ☐ safety

Review, Recycle, Remember

Incorporate the following items into your project files where appropriate.

- ■ Modals
- ■ Vocabulary and *In Words* related to health
- ■ Reflecting on readings
- ■ Agreeing or disagreeing
- ■ Opinion paragraphs

Reference Section

Part 1: Project Files

Part 2: Language Learning Skills and Strategies

Part 1: Project Files

Planning Your Project

1. How to Brainstorm

Brainstorming is an excellent strategy to generate ideas on your subject.

DO

- Write down as many thoughts and ideas as you can.
- Try to brainstorm together with your team members.
- Set a short time limit on this activity.

DON'T

- Judge or critique your ideas at this time.
- Worry about how to organize your ideas.

2. How to Prepare for Your Project

There are many ways you can prepare for your projects. The strategies below will help you get started on your project, do the necessary research, and then verify the content.

DO

- Research your subject on the Internet carefully.
- Type the words you are looking for (travel, tours, etc.) in a search engine. The more words you enter, the more specific your results will be.
- Narrow your search by adding more specific words (responsible travel, eco-tours,) if you get too many results.
- Check your spelling by using a dictionary or try searching with another word if you do not get any results.

DON'T

- Start your project until you read all the instructions carefully.
- Wait until the last minute to start your project or to ask for help.

3. How to Use the CARS Checklist to Validate Internet Sources

After you find an Internet site on your subject, verify if it is a source you can trust. One tool you can use is called the CARS checklist. Refer to page 148 for this helpful checklist.

Producing Your Project

1. How to Produce an Effective Oral Presentation

DO

- Think about the subject and get your ideas together. Refer to Unit 2, page 36.
- Take notes and prepare important ideas on cue cards in advance.
- Organize your ideas logically.
- Review speaking strategies from the book. Refer to Speaking Files, page 144.
- Consult the Pronunciation Files, page 142.
- Practise your presentation.

DON'T

- Memorize your presentation word for word.
- Write too much on your cue cards.

2. How to Write an Effective Paragraph

DO

- Determine the purpose of your paragraph (to give an opinion, to write a description, etc.).
- Write an effective topic sentence. Refer to Unit 3, page 56.
- Make sure your paragraph focuses on one central idea.
- Link your ideas together using transition words. Refer to Unit 4, page 74.

DON'T

- Write about more than one main idea per paragraph.
- Randomly connect sentences and include irrelevant details.
- Forget to review *Writing Files* when necessary.

3. How to Summarize

DO

- Become familiar with your subject.
- Think about the main message of the text.
- Summarize information into your own words by answering the questions: who, what, where, when, why, and how.

DON'T

- Write too little or too much.
- Add your own opinions or ideas when you summarize.
- Copy someone else's work—even if you only copy a few sentences or change a few words it is still considered plagiarism.

4. How to Write an Essay

An essay is made up of three main parts: the introduction, the body paragraphs, and the conclusion. Each part has a specific function. In addition, the thesis statement provides important information about the essay. The topic sentences provide the main information of each paragraph.

Essay Parts	Dos and Don'ts
Introduction • Introduces the subject and creates interest. • Includes a **thesis statement** which provides the main idea of the essay.	**Do** • Introduce the subject by using an anecdote, a quote, statistics, or historical information. • Grab the reader's attention. • Include a thesis statement. **Don't** • Start with the sentence, "I am going to talk about."
Body Paragraphs • Provide details which support the thesis statement. • Include a **topic sentence**, which provides the main idea of each paragraph.	**Do** • Write one topic sentence (main idea) per paragraph. • Connect ideas by using transition words. **Don't** • Include details that do not support your topic sentence.
Conclusion • Concludes the paragraph and summarizes the main points.	**Do** • Decide how you want to conclude the essay (with a prediction or a suggestion). • Use concluding words such as: *finally, to sum up, to conclude, in conclusion.* **Don't** • Repeat exact information from the text. • Introduce any new ideas.

Sample Essay

Introduction

Thesis Statement

Body Paragraphs
Topic Sentence

Topic Sentence

Conclusion
Topic Sentence

Gap Year

Some students are not yet ready for studies after secondary school and prefer to take a year off travelling and gaining experience. This is called a gap year. Taking a year off before college or university is common practice in European countries, like England. A gap year experience can change someone. There are many benefits to delaying studies in order to travel and learn. **A gap year can provide valuable experience for many students who need to take a year to discover themselves and the world.**

There are many reasons to consider a gap year, but mostly it allows a student to have extra time to make good career choices later. Some students just are not ready to make a decision about their careers at age 17 or 18 and the extra time could help them get to know themselves better. The stress of school might also prevent some students from wanting to continue with another three to four years of studies.

A year off travelling is not just a vacation, it can help students find work abroad and gain valuable real-life experience. There are many work options available, such as working as a ski or surfing instructor. Community work or volunteering are other ways to gain experience. Some people live on their own, while others prefer to stay with a family and work as an au pair or nanny. Exposure to a variety of cultures also helps people to expand their cultural knowledge and perspective.

There are numerous resources available on the Internet, if you want to learn more about taking a gap year. There are many websites with membership information and tips on how to travel safely during your gap year, including how to find a travel partner and which documents to bring. If someone is well-prepared, a gap year experience could be a positive experience.

Presenting and Evaluating Your Project

Now that you have your draft ready, there are some ways to verify your projects before you present them. Always read your draft and notes carefully and remember to consult the checklists below. Use your judgment accordingly as each project is different, which means not all the criteria will be relevant.

1. How to Present Written Work

The appearance of your project makes an impression on the reader. A correctly formatted and visually attractive document tells instructors that you put effort into your work.

DO

- Verify that all the instructions and requirements of the project have been completed.
- Type and double space your project.
- Begin with a title page that includes your name, the title of the project, etc.
- Use a standard 12-point font.
- Number your pages.
- Refer to How to Evaluate Your Project

DON'T

- Hand in your written work without checking and editing it.
- Wait until the last minute before asking your teacher for help or clarification.

2. How to Present a Successful Oral Project

You may have to present your ideas and research to a small group or to the class. Speaking in front of others can be a challenge, but it helps to be well-prepared.

DO

- Ask yourself if you can answer basic questions about the presentation.
- Look at the audience when you speak.
- Smile and relax.
- Learn the main points of your presentation.

DON'T

- Read your presentation.
- Memorize your entire presentation word for word.

3. How to Evaluate Your Project

Evaluate your own project or a classmate's project using the checklists below. Not every project will require all of these elements so use your own judgment.

Evaluate the Content

- ☐ Does the project have a clear purpose?
- ☐ Is the project interesting and creative?
- ☐ Is the project carefully planned and/or researched?
- ☐ Does the project show effort and participation by all the members of your team?
- ☐ Are the main ideas or arguments supported by facts?
- ☐ Does the project have an impact on the listener or reader?

Evaluate the Presentation and Organization

- ☐ Did you connect the ideas together by using transition words?
- ☐ Does the introduction include the theme or main point of the project?
- ☐ Does each paragraph contain a topic sentence?
- ☐ Is the project organised and easy to understand?

Evaluate the Language

- ☐ Do all sentences have a subject and a verb?
- ☐ Are the verbs formed correctly?
- ☐ Did you check the spelling of unfamiliar words?
- ☐ Does the vocabulary contain only English words?
- ☐ Did you try to use the vocabulary words from the unit?
- ☐ Is the language clear and easy to understand?

Part 2: Language Learning Skills and Strategies

Reading Files

1. How to Find the Main Idea (Unit 2)

The main idea of a text is the message the author wants you to understand. It is usually near the beginning of a text. The author often states the main idea more than once.

To find the main idea in a text:

- Ask yourself what message the author wants to send.
- Look for examples and anecdotes in the text. They support the main idea.

2. How to Skim and Scan (Unit 2)

When you **skim** a text, you read it quickly for specific information, such as the main idea. You do not need to read every word or stop to look up a word in the dictionary.

When you **scan** a text, you already know what you are looking for, such as a certain word, name, or date.

3. How to Read for Details (Unit 3)

Read a text more than once to fully understand it.

- Understand words that repeat. These are often important words.
- Look for words that are familiar to you.
- Read the vocabulary words defined in the margin.
- Use a dictionary for any other words you may not know.

4. How to Recognize Informal Language (Unit 3)

Sometimes people who chat online use incorrect grammar, spelling, and punctuation when they write quickly. Look at this example.

U
unfriend paige right now.

I'm
im serious.

I don't
i dont care if they request you.

S
say no.

5. How to Identify the Speaker in a Text (Unit 4)

DO

- Look for quotation marks "…" that come before and after something a person says.
- Look for words like *says*, *mentions*, and *reports* before or after the quotation.
  Smith says, I'm convinced there's something out there.

DON'T

- Rely on only quotation marks. Look for the person's name before or after the statement with words like *says*, *believes*, or *reported that*.
  Barbara Smith says it's what she's known to be true for years.

Vocabulary Builder Files

6. How to Highlight Essential Information (Unit 4)
When you read, it is important to highlight the main points and any important information. This helps you to summarize what you read.

- Make sure to read the text at least once before you highlight.

- Think about what was important in the text.

- Read the text a second time, and then highlight important information. You do not need to highlight every word in a sentence.

- When you finish, read the highlighted parts to see if they include the information you are looking for.

7. How to Interpret a Message (Unit 6)
Sometimes song lyrics or texts have hidden or unclear messages. How can you figure out their meanings?

- Read the title.

- Read the text more than once.

- Look for repeating words or themes.

- Check for new vocabulary words.

- Think of what the themes may represent or symbolize. Song lyrics are often about themes like love, hope, and life.

8. How to Reflect on Readings (Unit 7)
Reflect on a reading by looking over the important information in the text. Try to connect the information from the text to other readings or your own personal experience.

As you read:

- Ask yourself if the subject is familiar.

- Have you read other texts or heard about the same subject? How is it similar?

- Does it remind you of experiences from your own life?

- Reflecting will help you to talk about the reading and provide your own insight.

1. How to Identify Cognates (Unit 1)
Sometimes an English word looks like a word in another language and has a similar meaning. These words are cognates. About one third of English words come from French. Sometimes there are only minor differences in the spelling.

When you identify cognates, you can understand parts of a text without using a dictionary.

2. How to Recognize False Cognates (Unit 1)
Watch out for false cognates.

These are words that look similar but have different meanings.

*This hotel has no **vacancy**, so we have to spend the rest of our **vacation** in a youth hostel.*

Use a dictionary if you are not sure of the meaning of a word.

3. How to Support Your Statement (Unit 2)
Use **because** (cause) to support the statements you make in writing.

*For Jay, I recommend yoga or swimming **because** he's non-competitive.*

4. How to Choose the Correct Definition in a Dictionary (Unit 3)
Many words have more than one meaning in a dictionary. To choose the correct definition of a word, you must see the word in context. Read the words before and after the word you do not understand to help you choose the right definition.

Compare:
*I bought a **mouse** from the pet shop.*
*I bought a **mouse** for my computer.*

5. How to Get Meaning from Context (Unit 4)

DON'T

- Immediately use a dictionary to understand words you do not know in a text.

DO

- Guess what the word means by looking at it in context.
- Look at the new word to see if it looks like another word you know (**know**ledge).
- Identify the part of speech (noun, verb, etc.) to help understand its function.
- Look for words that you know before and after the new word to help you understand it.

Pronunciation Files

1. How to Pronounce the Third-Person Singular -S (Unit 1)

There are three possible ending sounds: /s/, /z/, and /iz/.

/s/	/z/	/iz/
looks	says	wishes
eats	flies	places
parks	sends	causes

2. How to Pronounce the Contracted Forms of the Present Progressive (Unit 2)

Look at the long forms and the contracted forms of the present progressive.

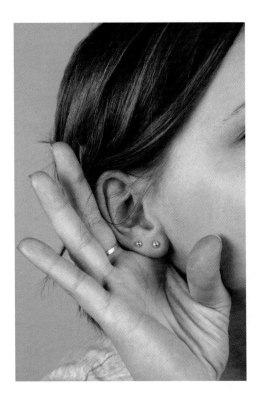

Long Form	Contraction
I am running.	I'm running.
You are training.	You're training.
He is canoeing.	He's canoeing.
She is skating.	She's skating.
We are boxing.	We're boxing.
They are dancing.	They're dancing.

Negative Long Form	Negative Contraction
I am not running.	I'm not running.
You are not training.	You're not training.
He is not canoeing.	He's not canoeing.
She is not skating.	She's not skating.
We are not boxing.	We're not boxing.
They are not dancing.	They're not dancing.

3. How to Pronounce the -ED Ending of Regular Verbs in the Simple Past (Unit 3)

There are three ways to pronounce regular verb endings in the past tense: /id/, /t/, or /d/.
These pronunciations are determined by the sound at the end of the verb to which the -ed ending was added.

Pronunciation of the Verb Ending in the Past Tense	Rules	Examples
/id/	Verbs that end in a /t/ or /d/ sound	created, respected, folded, landed
/t/	Verbs that end in a /f/, /p/, /k/, /s/, /sh/, /ch/, or /x/ sound	laughed, hopped, worked, passed, washed, watched, boxed
/d/	Verbs that end in all other sounds	robbed, lived, hugged, paged, filled, tuned

4. How to Pronounce Silent Letters (Unit 4)

Some words contain letters that we do not pronounce. Here are a few of the main ones. Look at the list of words with silent letters below.

Silent Letters	Words with Silent Letters
B	thumb, lamb, climb, plumber
G	sign, design
H	ghost, hour, honest
L	walk, talk, could, would
K	know, knee, knight, knife, knit
S	island
T	castle, whistle, listen, ballet, chalet, debut
W	write, who, wrist, wrong

5. How to Pronounce the Words Spelled with *EI* (Unit 5)

The *ei* vowel combination is usually pronounced /ay/ as in *day*, but there are some exceptions.
Each word below is paired with another word that has the same vowel sound.

Word Pairs

weight	neighbour	reign	beige	eight
way	navy	rain	bay	ate

6. How to Pronounce Words that Begin with the Letter *H* (Unit 6)

The *h-* in certain words is pronounced (as in *happy*) and in others it is silent (as in *honour*).
Some words that begin with *wh-* also have an /h/ sound (as in *who*).

7. How to Pronounce the /*TH*/ Sound (Unit 7)

The /th/ sound found in words like *health*, *think*, and *with* can be tricky to pronounce.
Make sure to differentiate this sound from the /t/ sound.
Try to stick out your tongue when you say /th/.

8. How to Pronounce *Can* or *Can't* (Unit 7)

Note the emphasis of *can* and *can't* within the sentence.
In speaking, *can't* is emphasized or stressed, but not *can*.

You **can't** use olive oil.
I can **get** fresh oregano.

Speaking Files

1. How to Make Introductions (Unit 1)
To introduce yourself:
Hi, my name is Sophia.
Hi, I'm Sam.
Let me introduce myself.

To introduce someone else:
This is Valerie.
Let me introduce you to Eric.

Responses:
Nice to meet you.
Pleased to meet you.

2. How to Use Help Strategies (Unit 2)
To ask how to say something in English:
How do you say quitter in English?

To ask how to spell a word:
How do you spell government?

To ask what a word means:
What does actually mean?

3. How to Express Pros and Cons (Unit 3)
Use the expressions in bold to express the positive and negative sides of an issue.

On the one hand, *cellphones help us to communicate easily.* **On the other hand,** *they cause a lot of interruptions.*

Cars are very useful. **For one thing,** *cars help us get somewhere fast.* **However,** *gas is very expensive.*

Although *debit cards are very easy to use, sometimes people lose them.*

4. How to Talk About Beliefs (Unit 4)
Use the following expressions in the simple present when discussing your beliefs.

I think that...
I really believe...
I don't believe...
Do you believe in...?
I agree.
I disagree with...
I am not convinced that...

Do you **believe** *in spirits?*
I don't **believe** *in ghosts, but*
I **believe that** *angels are around us.*

5. How to Talk About Perceptions (Unit 5)
Use the verbs *seem* or *appear* to talk about your perceptions.

It **seemed** *to me that he was not telling the truth.*
He **seemed** *to pause before speaking.*
She **appeared** *to be looking to the left.*

6. How to Avoid Overgeneralizations (Unit 5)
When you speak or write, accuracy and precision are important. Avoid overgeneralizations like *everyone*, *always*, or *never*, unless it is absolutely true.

Many *people lie on dating websites.* (~~Everyone~~ *lies...*)
Women **sometimes** *lie in their online profiles.* (*Women* ~~always~~ *lie...*)
Men **don't usually** *lie about their age.* (*Men* ~~never~~ *lie...*)

7. How to Emphasize Your Point (Unit 5)
Add information to support your statement by using these words or phrases: *actually, as a matter of fact, also, in fact.*

Christopher Reeves was a great actor; **in fact,** *he was an even greater role model after he became paraplegic.*

8. How to Ask for Clarification (Unit 6)
You may need to ask someone to repeat or clarify information. Practise these questions.

Could you repeat that, please?
What was that again?
I didn't understand what you said.
What did you say?
Did you mean that he won an award?

Grammar Files

9. How to Agree or Disagree with Someone (Unit 7)
To agree with someone's affirmative statement, use:
me too, so do I, I also...

*Yes, **so do I. I also** eat cereal for breakfast.*

To agree with someone's negative statement, use: *me neither; ...either.*

*I don't work **either**.*

10. How to Give Directions (Unit 7)
Use *at, on, until, along, in front of,* and *across from* for directions.

*Turn left **at** the stop sign.*
*Turn right **on** Wood Avenue.*
*Go straight **until** you reach the bakery.*
*Continue **along** Oak Street.*
*It's **at** the corner of Maple Road and Oak Street.*
*The bakery is **in front of** the bank.*
*The butcher is **across from** the deli.*

11. How to Express an Opinion (Unit 7)

DO

- Use the following opinion statements to express your thoughts:

  In my opinion,
  I believe that
  I don't think
  I am convinced that...

  ***I strongly believe** that we should reduce our carbon footprint.*

DON'T

- Use double pronouns.

  ~~Me,~~ *I think this diet works*

1. Simple Present (Unit 1)
Use the simple present to talk about facts, habits, and preferences.

Make sure to add *-s* or *-es* to regular verbs in the third person singular (*he, she,* or *it*).

Refer to Grammar Book, Unit 1.

2. Questions in the Simple Present (Unit 1)
Use the auxiliary *do* or *does* with the verb to make questions and negative statements in the simple present.

***Do** you like to cook?*
*No, I **don't**.*

***Does** he like pets?*
*No, he **doesn't**.*

Never use *do* or *does* with the verb *be*.

***Are** you neat? Yes, I **am**.*
***Is** she messy? No, she **isn't**.*

Refer to Grammar Book, Unit 1.

3. Present Progressive and *-ING* Nouns (Unit 2)
Use the present progressive to describe events taking place at the moment of speaking.

To form the present progressive, add *-ing* to the base form of the verb. Remember to add the auxiliary *be* or *are* before the verb.

*You **are** ska**ting** too fast.*
Watch out!

You can also use the *-ing* ending to form a noun.

***Skating** is a fun winter sport.*

Refer to Grammar Book, Unit 2.

4. Using an Apostrophe (Unit 2)
An apostrophe replaces a letter, or letters, in the contracted form of a word.

Write the apostrophe in the same place as the letter you removed.

He is training hard.
*He**'s** training for a competition.*

5. Expressions to Indicate the Past (Unit 3)
Use these expressions to talk about past actions and habits: *in those days, back then, before, a long time ago, used to.*

*People **used to** listen to music on cassette tapes **back then**.*
*Telegrams were sent **a long time ago**.*

Refer to Grammar Book, Unit 5.

6. Simple Past (Unit 3)

Use the simple past for actions in the past that are completely finished.

Regular verbs end in -d or -ed.

*They **lived** in an old house.*

Pay attention to irregular verbs.

*We **had** many old records when we **were** teenagers.*

Refer to Grammar Book, Unit 5.

7. Question Formation in the Simple Past (Unit 3)

To form questions in the simple past, use the auxiliary *did* and the base form of the verb.

*Why **did** she **disconnect**?*
(Why did she ~~disconnected~~?)

Do not use an auxiliary with the verb *be*.

*Where **were** you yesterday?*
(Where ~~did you were~~ yesterday?)

Refer to Grammar Book, Unit 5.

8. Using the Possessive 'S (Unit 4)

Add the *'s* to a word to show possession. Remember to put the apostrophe after the -s for words that end in -s.

*My friend**'s** book was in my parent**s'** house.*

Refer to Grammar Book, Unit 3.

9. Past Progressive (Unit 4)

Form the past progressive by using the auxiliary *was* or *were*, and the base form of the verb with an *-ing* ending.

*We **were watching** the show.*

The negative is formed by adding *not* after the auxiliary.

*He **was not listening** to my story.*

To make a question, place the auxiliary before the subject.

***Are** you **waiting** for us?*

Refer to Grammar Book, Unit 6.

10. Simple Past and Past Progressive (Unit 4)

Use the **past progressive** for an action that was in progress at a specific moment in the past or for a past action in progress that was interrupted.

Use the **simple past** for an action in the past that is completely finished.

*While I **was sleeping**, I **heard** a noise. The strange sounds **were coming** from the basement. I **got** out of bed and **went** downstairs.*

Refer to Grammar Book, Units 5 and 6.

11. *Worse, the Worst,* and *as Bad as* (Unit 5)

When you compare two things, use *worse*.

*Stealing is **worse** than lying.*

When you compare more than two things, use *the worst*.

***The worst** offence on the list is going over the speed limit.*

When two things are equally bad, use *as bad as*.

*I think getting help on an essay is **as bad as** cheating.*

Refer to Grammar Book, Unit 7.

12. Using *Than* in Comparisons (Unit 5)

Use *than* to compare two things.

*It is much **harder** to remember a lie **than** the truth.*

*People who are honest feel **more relaxed than** those who are lying.*

Make sure to spell *than* correctly. (~~then~~)

Refer to Grammar Book, Unit 7.

13. Comparatives and Superlatives (Unit 5)

Words with one or two syllables usually add -er and -est endings to form the comparative and the superlative.

light
*light**er**: Comparative*
*light**est**: Superlative*

Words with more than two syllables usually use the words *more* and *most*.

exciting
***more** exciting: Comparative*
***most** exciting: Superlative*

Refer to Grammar Book, Unit 7.

14. Adverbs (Unit 6)

Adverbs explain how something is done. They also modify an adjective.

*The fundraiser was **really** successful.*
(describes how successful the fundraiser was)

To form adverbs, you usually add *-ly* to an adjective.
*quick → quick**ly***
*endless → endless**ly***

Note: The adverb form of *good* is *well*.

*She speaks English **well**.*

Refer to Grammar Book, Unit 7.

15. Future (Unit 6)

For possible future events or predictions, use *will* or *be going to*.

*He **will** probably **give** all the money to charity.* (possible future event)
*We **are going to be** very famous one day.* (prediction)

For planned or definite future events, use *be going to*.

*What **are** you **going to do** with the award money?* (planned future event)

Note: The contraction of *will not* is *won't*.

*He **won't apply** for the award this year.*

Refer to Grammar Book, Unit 8.

16. Uncountable Nouns (Unit 6)

Some clothing, like shorts, pants, and jeans are usually counted in pairs. Note the final *-s* in shorts.

*one pair of short**s***

Note: The word pair takes a final *-s* in the plural form.

*two pair**s** of jeans*

Refer to Grammar Book, Unit 3.

17. Modals (Unit 7)

Use modals before verbs to make suggestions or recommendations.

*Students **should** plan their days better.*
*He **could** pack a lunch the night before.*

Note there is no *-s* after the main verb. (could pack~~s~~)

Refer to Grammar Book, Unit 10.

18. Negative Modals (Unit 7)

Add *not* after the modal to make it negative.

*You **should not** smoke.* (suggestion)
*We **must not** be late.* (obligation)

When *have to* is in the negative form, it is not an obligation, but an option.

*You **have to** eat healthy!* (obligation)
*You **don't have to** finish your plate, if you don't want to.* (option)

Refer to Grammar Book, Unit 10.

19. Countable and Uncountable Nouns (Unit 7)

Some nouns are **countable**. Add *-s* or *-es* for the plural form.

*You should eat your bean**s**!*

Uncountable nouns do not take an *-s*. Use *some* or *much* to talk about quantity.

*Could you buy **some** milk?*
*There isn't **much** left.*

Refer to Grammar Book, Unit 3.

CARS Checklist

	What to Validate	Questions to Ask Yourself
1. Credibility	Find out if the source is credible, or if you can trust it.	Is the author respectable and well-known? Does the author have credentials?
	Look for a reliable website and the person who wrote the material (institution, contact information, etc.).	Does the website include the author's contact information? Is the information poorly written with a lot of mistakes?
2. Accuracy	Make sure the article is up to date, detailed, and contains all the facts (the whole truth).	Is there a date? Do you know when it was last modified?
	Make sure you know which audience the source is intended to reach.	Is the source intended for college students or higher?
	Look for information presented on both sides of an issue (unbiased).	Does the author present both sides of an issue?
3. Reasonableness	Make sure this is fair and objective information.	Is it very emotional writing? For example, a vegetarians' association stating that eating meat is bad for you is probably biased. Does it make skeptical claims? For example, a miracle cure for a problem should be approached with caution.
4. Support	Look for many sources that agree.	Can you find three sources that agree?
	Find sources that at least give similar information.	
	Do not rely on one source only or the first source that pops up.	

Words from the Academic Word List

Unit 1	Unit 2	Unit 3	Unit 4	Unit 5	Unit 6	Unit 7
to involve yourself	to create	to achieve available	an author to convince to emphasize to reveal	integrity	a goal to react a trend	to require